SUZUKI GT380

A COMPILATION OF 3 FACTORY MANUALS

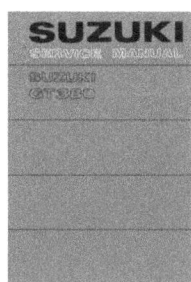

SERVICE MANUAL

DISC BRAKE SERVICE MANUAL

VM24SC CARBURETOR MANUAL

1972   **1977**

A Floyd Clymer Publication - 2025 VelocePress.com

PREFACE

TRADEMARKS & COPYRIGHT

SUZUKI® is the registered trademark of the SUZUKI MOTOR CO., LTD. and this publication is not sponsored by or endorsed by the trademark owner. We recognize that some words, model names and designations, for example, mentioned herein are the property of the trademark holder. We use them for identification purposes only. This is not an official publication however; it may include non-copyright works of the trademark holder.

INTRODUCTION

Welcome to the world of digital publishing ~ the book you now hold in your hand was printed using the latest state of the art digital technology. The advent of print-on-demand has forever changed the publishing process, never has information been so accessible and it is our hope that this book serves your informational needs for years to come. If this is your first exposure to digital publishing, we hope that you are pleased with the results. Many more titles of interest to the classic automobile and motorcycle enthusiast, collector and restorer are available via our website at www.VelocePress.com. We hope that you find this title as interesting as we do.

NOTE FROM THE PUBLISHER

The information presented is true and complete to the best of our knowledge. All recommendations are made without any guarantees on the part of the author or the publisher, who also disclaim all liability incurred with the use of this information.

INFORMATION ON THE USE OF THIS PUBLICATION

This manual is an invaluable resource for those interested in performing their own maintenance. However, in today's information age we are constantly subject to changes in common practice, new technology, availability of improved materials and increased awareness of chemical toxicity. As such, it is advised that the user consult with an experienced professional prior to undertaking any procedure described herein. While every care has been taken to ensure correctness of information, it is obviously not possible to guarantee complete freedom from errors or omissions or to accept liability arising from such errors or omissions. Therefore, any individual that uses the information contained within, or elects to perform or participate in do-it-yourself repairs or modifications acknowledges that there is a risk factor involved and that the publisher or its associates cannot be held responsible for personal injury or property damage resulting from the use of the information or the outcome of such procedures.

WARNING!

One final word of advice, this publication is intended to be used as a reference guide, and when in doubt the reader should consult with a qualified technician.

www.VelocePress.com

IMPORTANT INFORMATION REGARDING PAGE NUMBERS

Each of the three manuals included in this publication have their own index. The page numbers that correspond to each individual index are printed to the bottom of each page.

The page numbers printed to the top of each page are the page numbers within the book to enable quick access to each of the three individual manuals. They are referenced below:

Book page number 1   SERVICE (WORKSHOP) MANUAL

Book page number 57   DISC BRAKE MANUAL

Book Page number 85   VM24SC CARBURETOR MANUAL

SUZUKI SERVICE MANUAL

MODEL

SERVICE GUIDE

FOREWORD

This Service Manual provides you with the necessary information in the maintenance work of SUZUKI Model GT380.

Unlike its predecessors, GT380 is mounted with a three cylinder engine having increased cooling capacity during continuous high speed riding by adopting SUZUKI's own RAM AIR SYSTEM for the engine cooling method; it is a high-speed motorcycle with a smooth running engine with excellent acceleration. In order to maintain its excellent performance, the users must be encouraged to have their machines checked regularly. It is also necessary for service men to be well trained in the maintenance work particularly of the new mechanisms, including the installation of cylinder head, adjustment of carburetor and the correction of the ignition timing, etc.

It is hoped that this Service Manual will help each service man to provide better servicing works to the users utilizing his already accumulated skills.

SUZUKI MOTOR CO., LTD.
Export service section

CONTENTS

		Page
1.	SPECIFICATIONS	3
2.	PERFORMANCE CURVES	5
3.	TIPS ON OPERATION	6
4.	SPECIAL TOOLS	7
5.	TROUBLE SHOOTING	9
6.	ENGINE	13
6-1.	Removing engine from frame	13
6-2.	Cylinder head	17
6-3.	Cylinder	18
6-4.	Piston pin	18
6-5.	Piston ring	19
6-6.	Piston	20
6-7.	Oil pump	22
6-8.	Removing alternator	24
6-9.	Contact breaker	24
6-10.	Servicing of contact breaker cam shaft	25
6-11.	Crank case right cover	25
6-12.	Clutch	27
6-13.	Primary pinion and breaker cam shaft drive gear	30
6-14.	Crank case	30
6-15.	Transmission	31
6-16.	Kick starter mechanism	34
6-17.	Crankshaft	35
6-18.	Suzuki Recycle Injection System	35
6-19.	Oil seal	36
6-20.	Bearing	36
7.	CARBURETOR	37
7-1.	Specifications	37
7-2.	Overhauling carburetor	38
7-3.	Adjusting carburetor	38
7-4.	Adjusting fuel level	40
7-5.	Inspecting float chamber parts	40
7-6.	Overflowing	41
7-7.	Attaching carburetor	41
8.	ENGINE ELECTRICAL EQUIPMENT	42
8-1.	Alternator	42
8-2.	Ignition system	45
8-3.	Condenser capacity and ignition coil resistance	45
9.	BODY	46
9-1.	Front fork	46
9-2.	Brake	46
9-3.	Drive chain	47
9-4.	Removing rear wheel	48
9-5.	Tire	48
10.	TIGHTENING TORQUE	49
11.	IMPORTANT FUNCTIONAL PARTS	50
*	PERIODICAL INSPECTION LIST	51
*	WIRING DIAGRAM	52
*	EXPLODED VIEW OF ENGINE	53

LEFT & RIGHT SIDE VIEWS

1. SPECIFICATIONS

◆ Dimensions and Weight

Overall length	2,105 mm (82.9 in)
Overall width	850 mm (33.5 in)
Overall height	1,100 mm (43.3 in)
Wheelbase	1,355 mm (53.4 in)
Ground clearance	155 mm (6.1 in)
Tires front	3.00 - 19 4PR
rear	3.50 - 18 4PR
Dry weight	171 kg (377 lbs)

◆ Performance

Maximum speed	168-176 kph (105-110 mph)
Acceleration (0-400 m)	13.8 sec
Braking distance	14 m (46.0 ft) @50 kph (30 mph)

◆ Engine

Type	2-cycle, ram air cooling, piston valve engine
Cylinder	Three, aluminum
Bore x stroke	54 x 54 mm (2.13 x 2.13 in)
Piston displacement	371 cc (22.6 cu-in)
Corrected compression ratio	6.7 : 1
Maximum horse power	38 hp/7,500 rpm
Maximum torque	3.93 kg-m (28.4 lb-ft)/6,000 rpm
Starter	Kick lever

◆ Fuel system

Carburetor	Three, VM24SC
Air cleaner	Wet polyurethane filter
Fuel tank capacity	15.0 ltr (4.0/3.3 gal, US/Imp) including 4.6 ltr (1.2/1.0 gal, US/Imp) of reserve

◆ Lubrication system

Engine	SUZUKI CCI
Gearbox	Oil bath, 1,400 cc (3.0/2.5 pt, US/Imp)
Oil tank capacity	1.5 ltr (3.2/2.6 pt, US/Imp)

◆ Ignition system

Ignition	Battery
Ignition timing	$24°\,^{+3°}_{-3°}\,(3.00\,^{+0.76}_{-0.48}\,\text{mm})$ B.T.D.C.
Spark plug	NGK B-7ES or Nippon Denso W-22ES

◆ Transmission

Clutch		Wet multi-disc
Gearbox		6 speeds, constant mesh
Gear shifting		Left foot operated, return change
Primary reduction ratio		2.833 : 1 (68/24)
Final reduction ratio		3.000 : 1 (42/14)
Gear ratios	low	2.333 : 1 (28/12)
	second	1.500 : 1 (24/16)
	third	1.157 : 1 (22/19)
	fourth	0.904 : 1 (19/21)
	fifth	0.782 : 1 (18/23)
	top	0.708 : 1 (17/24)
Overall reduction ratios		
	low	19.82 : 1
	second	12.74 : 1
	third	9.83 : 1
	fourth	7.68 : 1
	fifth	6.64 : 1
	top	6.01 : 1

◆ Suspension system

Front suspension	Telescopic fork with hydraulic damper
Rear suspension	Swinging arm with hydraulic damper

◆ Steering

Steering angle	40° (right & left)
Caster	62°
Trail	109 mm (4.3 in)
Turning radius	2.3 m (7.5 ft)

◆ Brakes

Front brake	Mechanical, 2 leading shoes
Rear brake	Mechanical, leading trading shoes

◆ Electrical equipment

Generator	Alternator
Battery	12V 7AH
Head lamp	12V 35/25W
Tail/brake lamp	12V 8/23W
Neutral indicator lamp	12V 3.4W
Speedometer lamp	12V 3.4W
High beam indicator lamp	12V 3.4W
Tachometer lamp	12V 3.4W
Turn signal lamp	12V 23W
Turn signal indicator lamp	12V 1.7W
Fuse	15A

Specifications subject to change without notice.

2. PERFORMANCE CURVES

ENGINE PERFORMANCE

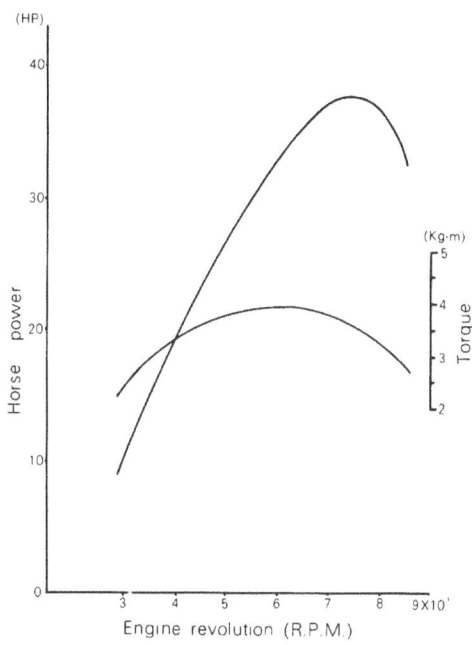

MOTORCYCLE PERFORMANCE

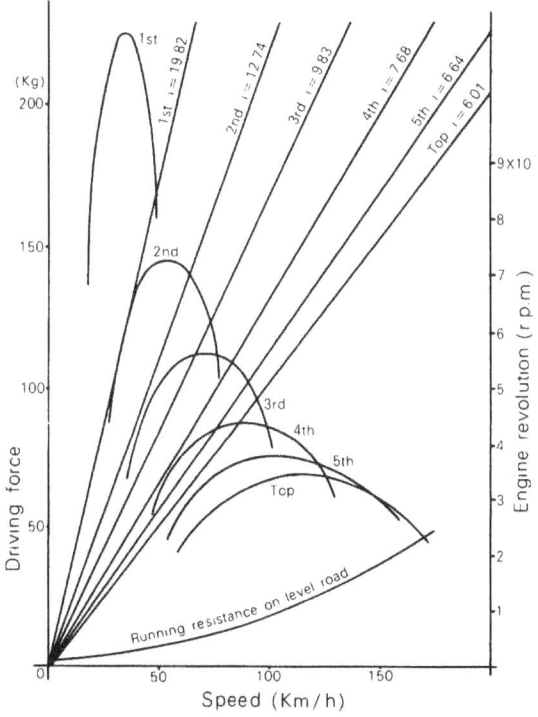

3. TIPS ON OPERATION

To keep the motorcycle in peak condition, please advise your customers to follow these tips and this will give top performance at all times.

3-1. Breaking-in

The life of the motorcycle depends on the breaking-in of the engine and the way in which the motorcycle is treated. Therefore, breaking-in with best care is much important to prevent excessive wear of the parts and noise and to prolong the engine life. During the breaking-in period, do not operate the motorcycle at high speed nor allow the engine to run wide open. Keep to specified breaking-in speed limits. Gradually raise the speed as the covered mileage increases.

　　　　First 500 miles (800 km) . . . . Below 4,000 R.P.M.
　　　　up to 1,000 miles (1,600 km) . . . . Below 5,000 R.P.M.

3-2. Fuel and oil

The engine's moving parts such as crankshaft, crankshaft bearings, con-rod, piston and cylinder wall are positively lubricated by fresh oil which is separately pressure-delivered from the variable displacement oil pump. This unique force oiling system is called "SUZUKI CCI". Put gasoline only in the fuel tank and lubrication oil in the oil tank. Recommended fuel and oil are as follows.

　　　FUEL . . . . REGULAR GRADE GASOLINE
　　　OIL . . . . SUZUKI CCI OIL

* If Suzuki CCI oil is not available, non-diluent (non-self mixing type) two stroke oil with around SAE #30 may be used.

3-3. Genuine parts

When replacing parts, always use genuine Suzuki parts, which is precision-made under severe quality controls. If imitation parts (not genuine parts) are used, good performance cannot be expected from the motorcycle and in the worst case, they can cause a breakdown.

4. SPECIAL TOOLS

Special tools listed here are used to disassemble, assemble and perform other maintenance and service. These special tools make work easy which cannot be done simply with ordinary tools.
It is recomended to provide these special tools as a shop equipment.

Ref.No.	Tool No.	Tool name
1	09910–10710	8mm stud installing tool
2	09910–11510	10mm stud installing tool
3	09910–20113	Piston holder
4	09920–51510	Clutch sleeve hub holder
5	09920–60310	Clutch sleeve hub holder handle
6	09920–70111	Snap ring opener (small)
7	09913–50110	Oil seal remover
8	09913–61110	Bearing puller
9	09913–70122	Bearing and oil seal installing tool
10	09913–80111	Bearing and oil seal installing tool
11	09930–10111	Spark plug wrench
12	09930–20111	Point wrench with 0.35 mm gauge
13	09930–33310	Rotor remover (for KOKUSAN)
14	09930–50951	Rotor remover (for DENSO)
15	09931–00112	Timing gauge
16	09940–10122	Steering stem lock nut wrench
17	09940–60112	Spoke nipple wrench
18	09900–07403	T-type cross head screw driver (for 6mm screw)
19	09900–09002	Shock driver
20	09900–06103	Snap ring remover
21	09900–21802	Chain joint tool
22	09900–27002	Timing tester
23	09900–25001	Pocket tester
24	09900–28102	Electro tester
25	09900–28401	Hydrometer

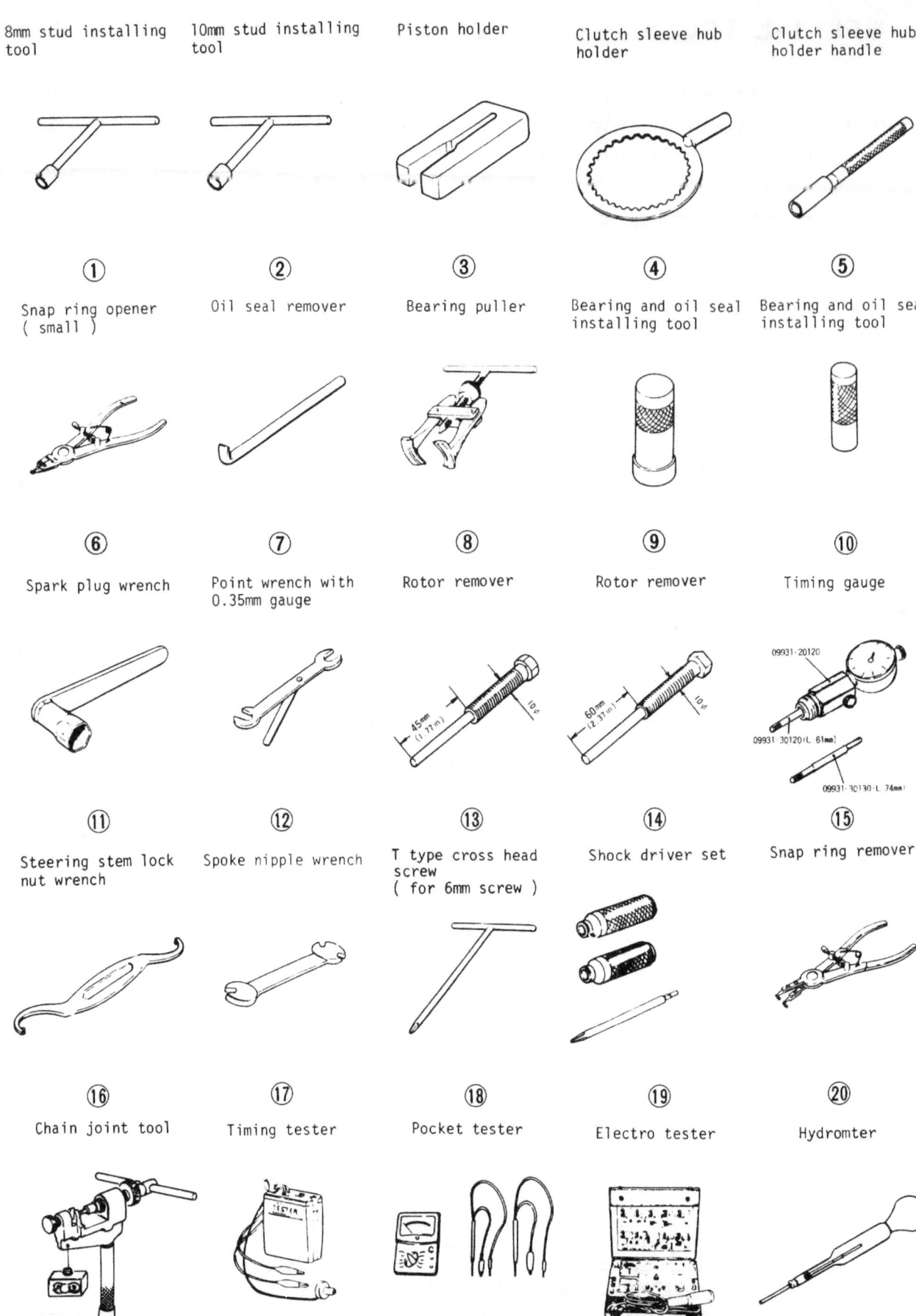

5. TROUBLE SHOOTING

When trouble occurs with a motorcycle, it is important to find the source of the trouble as rapidly as possible. It is also necessary to perform only the work required to repair the machine without bothering with parts which are functioning correctly. The list of possible troubles and their causes given below should help the service man to repair motorcycles quickly without loss of effort.

5-1. If engine is hard to start

Check fuel in the fuel tank first. When a proper amount of fuel is in the tank, check the following points.

Order and Description	Check Points	Remedy
1. Check to see that fuel flows into carburetor	* If fuel does not enter into carburetor	
	1. Fuel strainer clogged	Remove and clean
	2. Fuel pipe clogged or damaged	Clean or replace
	3. Tank cap air vent clogged	Clean with wire
	4. Fuel cock clogged	Clean
2. Check to see that spark jumps in spark plug. (Turn engine with kick starter).	* If blue or hot spark jumps in the spark plug, check the following points.	
	1. Ignition timing	Adjust
	2. Carburetion	Adjust
	3. Engine compression	Recover it
	* If spark is weak	
	1. Damage in spark plug	Replace
	2. Incorrect spark plug gap	Adjust
	3. Damage in spark plug cap	Replace
	4. Dirty contact points	Clean and adjust
	5. Bad insulation in condenser	Replace
	6. Damage in ignition coil	Replace
	* If there is no spark	
	1. Damage in spark plug	Replace
	2. Dirty or wet spark plug	Clean
	3. Incorrect spark plug gap	Adjust
	4. Dirty or incorrect contact point gap	Clean and adjust
	5. Bad insulation in condenser	Replace
	6. Damage in ignition coil or primary coil	Replace
	7. Damage in ignition switch	Replace
	8. Damage in wiring harness	Repair or replace
	9. Incorrect spark plug heat range	Replace

3. Check to see that engine compression is proper (Turn engine with kick starter).	* If engine compression is improper	
	1. Cylinder and piston rings worn	Repair or replace
	2. Piston ring stick on piston	Repair or replace
	3. Cylinder head gasket damaged	Replace
	4. Cylinder base gasket damaged	Replace
	5. Piston damaged	Replace
	6. Spark plug improperly tightened	Tighten securely
	7. Spark plug gasket faded	Replace
	8. Cylinder head improperly tightened	Tighten securely
	9. Gas leakage from crankcase	Repair or replace
	10. Cylinder or cylinder head damaged	Replace
	11. Oil seals damaged	Replace

5−2. **If abnormal noise is heard in engine**

	Check Points	Remedy
	1. Too big clearance between piston and cylinder	Repair or replace
	2. Too big clearance between piston rings and grooves	Replace piston
	3. Piston rings stiff with carbon	Clean
	4. Con-rod big end worn	Replace
	5. Con-rod small end bearing worn	Replace
	6. Piston rings damaged	Replace
	7. Ignition timing too advanced	Adjust
	8. Defective primary pinion and gear	Replace
	9. Crankshaft bearings worn	Replace
	10. Defective transmission gear	Replace
	11. Defectibe transmission bearings	Replace

5−3. **If engine overheats**

If engine overheats at high speed running after it is broken in, check to see if the oiling system is in good condition, the brake is dragging, or cylinder cooling fins are dirty. Inspect the following points.

Description	Check Points	Remedy
1. Check to see if oiling system functions properly.	1. Improperly adjusted oil pump control lever	Adjust
	2. Air in oil lines	Remove air
	3. Oil tank cap breather hole clogged.	Repair
	4. Incorrect oil used	Use prescribed oil

2. Check to see if engine compression is higher than standard	* Too high compression 1. Carbon deposits in combustion chamber 2. Too thin cylinder head gasket	Remove carbon deposit Replace
3. Check carbon deposit	* Check carbon deposit in muffler, exhaust pipe, exhaust port and combustion chamber	Disassemble and remove carbon deposit
4. Check to see that piston rings move smoothly in grooves	* Piston rings stiff by carbon deposit	Remove carbon deposit
5. Check to see that the clutch works properly	Clutch slippage	Adjust
6. Check to see that the ignition timing is correct		Adjust
7. Drive chain too tight		Adjust
8. Incorrect spark plug heat range		Replace with colder plug
9. Too lean fuel mixture		Adjust carburetor

5-4. Defective clutch

Description	Check Points	Remedy
1. Clutch slippage	1. Improperly adjusted clutch 2. Clutch springs worn 3. Clutch plates worn	Adjust Replace Replace
2. If clutch drags	1. Improper weight oil 2. Uneven clutch spring tension	Replace Replace

5-5. Gear shifting troubles

1. Description	Check Points	Remedy
1. Gear engagement	* If gears do not engage 1. Gear shifting cam groove damaged 2. Gear shifting forks not moved smoothly on cam 3. Gear shifting fork damaged 4. Gears seized	Replace shifting cam Rectify with emery paper Replace Replace
2. Gear shifting lever	* If gear shifting lever does not return to normal positon.	

	1. Gear shifting shaft return spring damaged	Replace
	2. Friction between gear shifting shaft and crankcase	Repair bent shaft or replace
3. Jumping out of gear	* If the gears disengage while running.	
	1. Gear shifting fork worn or bent	Replace
	2. Gear dog teeth worn	Replace gear
	3. Gear shifting cam worn or damaged	Repair bent shaft or replace

5-6. Bad stability and steering

Description	Check Points	Remedy
1. Handlebar is stiff	1. Steering stem lock nut tight	Adjust
	2. Steering stem bent	Repair or replace
	3. Steel balls damaged	Replace
2. Handlebar is not stable	1. Incorrect wheel alignment	Replace
	2. Play in front wheel fitting	Repair
	3. Steel balls damaged	Replace
	4. Fork stem bent	Repair or replace
	5. Bearing races worn or damaged	Repalce
	6. Front fork bent	Repair or replace
	7. Swinging arm bent	Repair
	8. Fork spring worn	Repalce
3. Wheel is not true	1. Incorrect wheel balance	Adjust
	2. Up-and-down play in hub bearings	Replace
	3. Wheel rim deformed	Repair or replace
	4. Loose spokes	Repair
	5. Chain too tight	Adjust
	6. Loose swinging arm fitting	Tighten
	7. Frame warped	Replace
	8. Incorrect tire pressure	Correct

6. ENGINE

6−1. Removing engine from frame

Prior to the removal operation, throughly clean the engine with a steam cleaner or cleaning solvent to remove road dirt.
The removal procedure is as follow.

Fig. 6−1−1 Disconnecting fuel pipe

Fig. 6−1−2 Removing fuel tank

Fig. 6−1−3 Disconnecting high tension cord

Fig. 6−1−4 Disconnecting alternator wires

Fig. 6−1−5 Disconnecting breaker wires

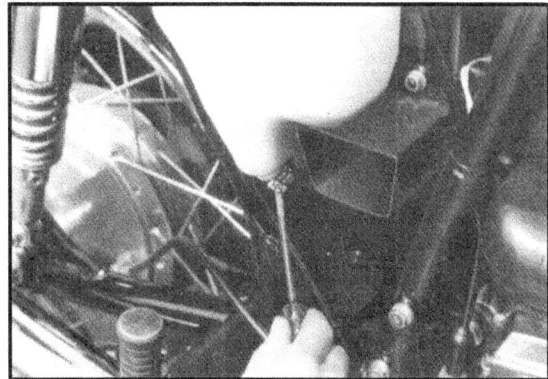

Fig. 6−1−6 Disconnecting oil pipe

Fig. 6-1-7 Removing left carburetor

Fig. 6-1-8 Removing air cleaner

Fig. 6-1-9 Removing center & right carburetor

Fig. 6-1-10 Removing oil pump cover

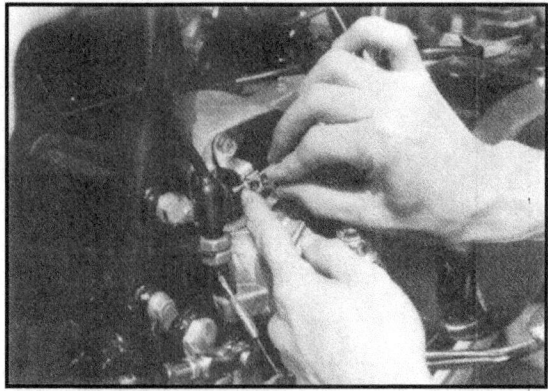

Fig. 6-1-11 Disconnecting oil pump control cable

Fig. 6-1-12 Disconnecting oil pump control cable

Fig. 6-1-13 Removing tachometer cable

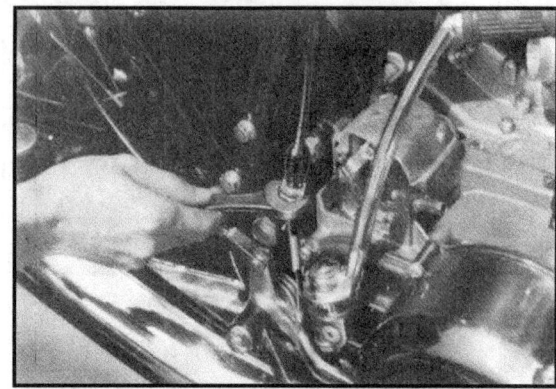

Fig. 6-1-14 Removing rear brake lamp switch

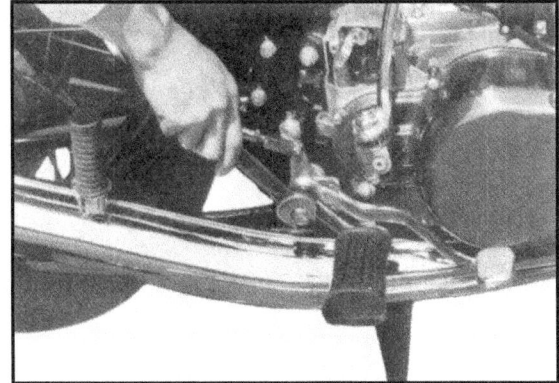

Fig. 6-1-15 Removing right front footrest

Fig. 6-1-16 Removing rear brake pedal

Fig. 6-1-17 Removing exhaust pipe clamp

Fig. 6-1-18 Removing pillion footrest

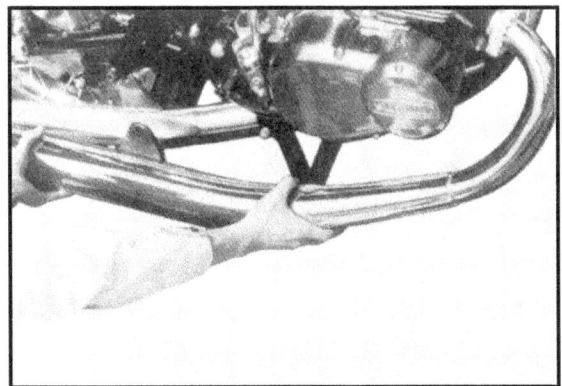

Fig. 6-1-19 Removing right & left muffler

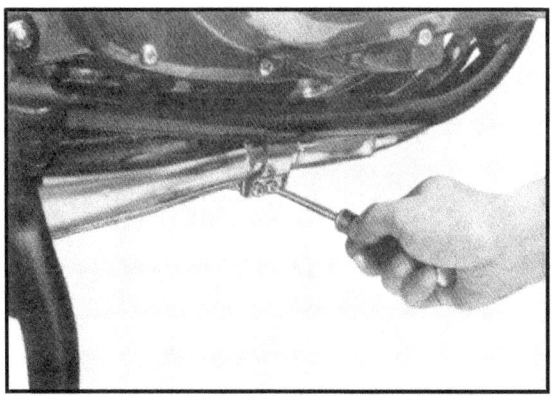

Fig. 6-1-20 Loosening muffler connector clamp

Fig. 6-1-21 Removing center muffler

Fig. 6-1-22 Removing left front footrest

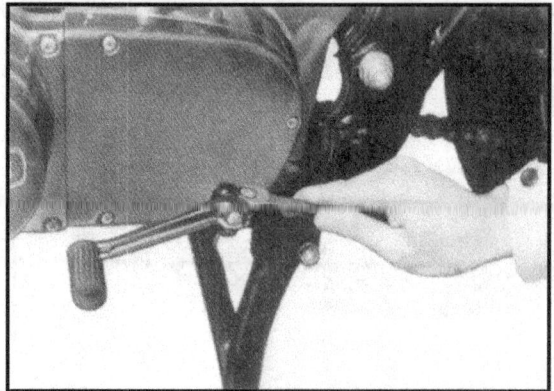

Fig. 6-1-23 Removing gear shift lever

Fig. 6-1-24 Removing engine sprocket outer cover

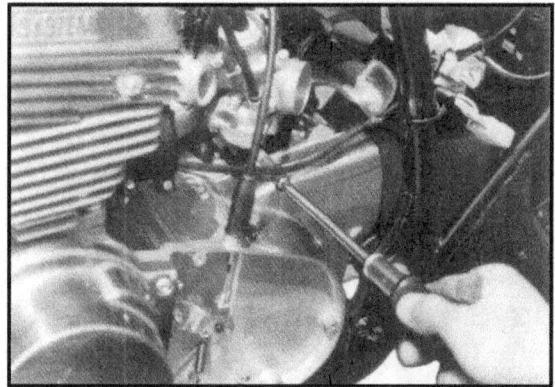

Fig. 6-1-25 Removing engine sprocket inner cover

Fig. 6-1-26 Removing engine sprocket

Fig. 6-1-27 Removing RAM AIR cover

Fig. 6-1-28 Removing engine mounting plate

Fig. 6-1-29 Removing engine mounting bolts

6-2. Cylinder head

1. Removing and installing cylinder head

   The cylinder head of this three cylinder engine has a solid structure being fixed with 12 cylinder head set nuts. In loosening and tightening these nuts, you should strictly observe the regular sequence as shown in Fig. 6-2-1. This is needed to avoid any distortion in the cylinder head at the time of an overhaul. Retightening of the cylinder head setting nuts must be carried out after the first 1,000km (750mi), then after that at every 3,000km (2,000mi).

   *Tightening torque of cylinder head set nuts is 350kg-cm (26 lb-ft)

   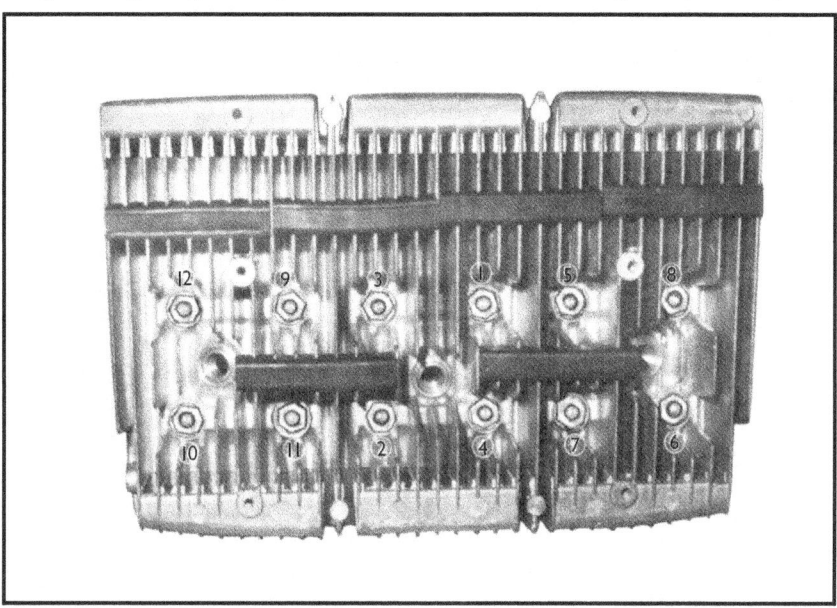

   Fig. 6-2-1 Cylinder head set nuts tightening order

2. Inspection and servicing

   1) Removing carbon

      Deposited carbons on the combustion chamber of the cylinder head will cause abnormal combustion and the overheating. Therefore, the deposited carbon must be removed after every 6,000 km (4,000mi) of running.

      Caution: In removing the carbon deposit, take care not to scratch the inner surface of the combustion chamber.

      If scratched, polish the parts with sand paper.

   2) Checking warp

      Since this cylinder head is a solid structure, due care is needed to prevent the warp of the surface because of a possible leakage of fuel-air mixture through the cylinder head. In fitting the cylinder unit (cylinder and cylinder head), be sure to check the surface level first. Adjust the level to it when needed, and install it after the level check. In case the gasket has been stuck onto the cylinder, remove it completely and then replace it with a new gasket.

      Level adjustment limit of each cylinder 0.03mm
      Relative warp limit to other cylinders   0.1mm
      Level limit of the whole unit   0.15mm

      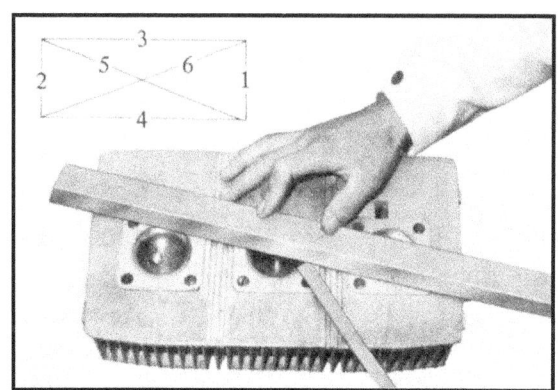

      Fig. 6-2-2 Positions when checking the warp

6-3. Cylinder

1. Checking

    Check the cylinder wear by using a cylinder gauge. As Fig. 6-3-1 shows, measurements must be taken at 6mm (0.24in) below the upper surface of the cylinder, 5mm (0.20in) above the exhaust port and 5mm (0.20in) below the inlet port, two times at each level in longitudinal and lateral directions. If the difference between the largest and the smallest values of the six times of the measurements is over 0.1mm (0.004in) the cylinder must be bored. After boring the cylinder, be sure to chamber the edge of each port. SUZUKI provides you with oversize pistons and piston rings (oversizes of 0.5mm and 1.0mm).

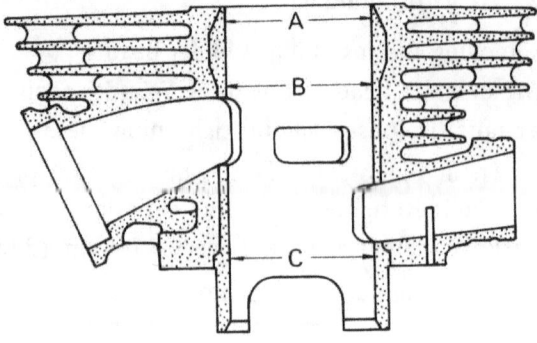

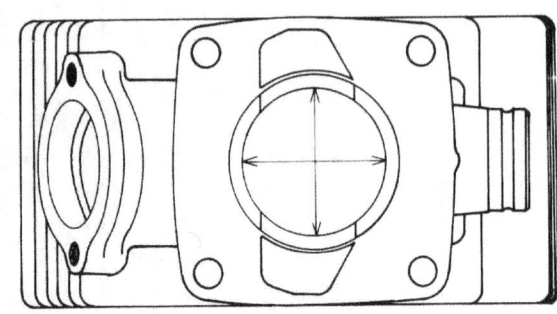

Fig. 6-3-1 Points to be measured

2. Removing carbon

    The accumulation of carbon is the most in places where the exhaust gas undergoes a most abrupt change. Also any motorcycle running at low speeds or with a defective engine tends to accelerate the carbon deposit. Check after every 6,000km (4,000 mi) of running and remove the carbon deposit if it exists. In the cylinder the carbon accumulates most at the exhaust port (see Fig. 6-3-2). Remove the carbon using a plain head screw driver or the equivalent. After all, you must take the utmost care not to make scratches on the cylinder wall when you remove the carbon.

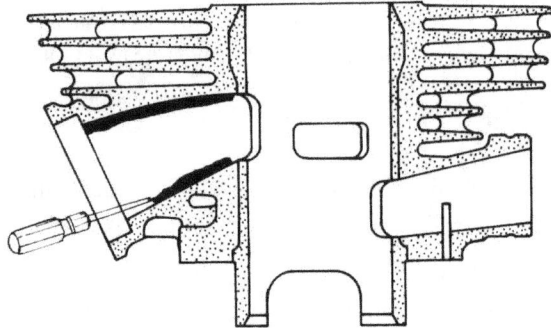

Fig. 6-3-2 Removing carbon deposit

6-4. Piston pin

Checking

The middle part of the piston pin functions as the inner race of the needle roller bearing, and the both ends makes a rubbing contact with the piston. Therefore, even a small size of defects on the piston pin will cause wear in the piston and the connecting rod. So check to see if there is any defect or wear in those parts whenever you disassemble them.

6–5. Piston ring

1. Removing piston ring

   Separate the joining ends of a piston ring with both thumbs, and take the ring off from the opposite side of the ring ends first.

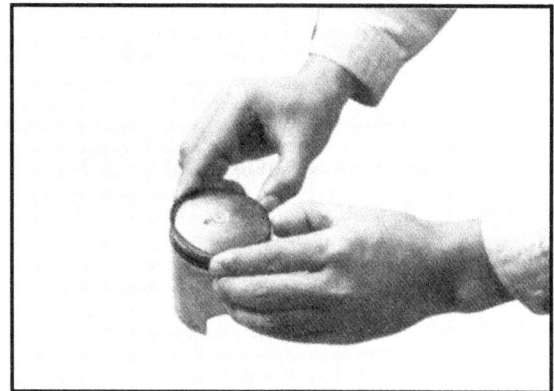

Fig. 6–5–1 Removing piston ring

2. Measuring wear

   Insert the piston ring to the bottom of cylinder, using the piston skirt so that the ring may be placed perpendicular to the cylinder wall. Next, measure the gap between the ends of the inserted piston ring, and if it exceeds the limiting value, the ring has to be replaced.

	Standard	Limit
Piston ring end gap	0.15 - 0.35mm (0.0059-0.0138in)	1.0mm (0.04in)

Fig. 6–5–2 Inserting piston ring into cylinder

3. Hints for fitting piston rings
   1) When fitting piston rings to piston

      Fit piston rings onto the piston in the reverse order used in "removing" after the washing.

Fig. 6–5–3 Measuring end gap

* Warp

When piston rings are fitted around the piston, rotate the rings to check. If any foreign materials are found between them, it does not rotate too smoothly. In that case, wash them again before fitting the rings.

Because strain induces warp as shown in Fig. 6-5-4, the piston ring should not be forced in.

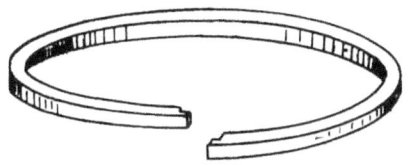

Fig. 6–5–4 Twisted piston ring

* Top side and bottom side of rings

Keystone type ring and the flat ring are used for the first and the second ring of GT380, respectively; therefore, the first and the second ring can not be interchanged.

The top side of these piston rings have letter markings, so make sure that they are on the top when you fit the rings.

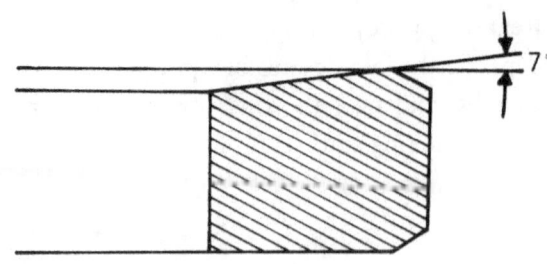

Fig. 6-5-5 Keystone type piston ring

2) When fitting piston into cylinder

In inserting a piston into cylinder, you may feel some resistance due to the tension of the piston rings. Also, unless the piston ring ends are not aligned to the knock pin position, you can not insert the piston into the cylinder. Do not try to insert it forcibly, otherwise the piston rings will be broken.

6-6. Piston

1. Inspecting and repairing

    1) Clearance between piston and cylinder

    A standard clearance between piston and cylinder is 0.045mm (0.0018in). The clearance denotes here the difference between the inner bore diameter of cylinder and the outer diameter of piston. In this case, the cylinder bore denotes the dimension measured at 20mm (0.79 in) below the upper surface of the cylinder in the transverse direction, and the piston diameter is the one measured at 26mm (1.02in) above the piston skirt in the direction perpendicular to the piston pin hole.

    2) Checking piston pin hole

    Insert a piston pin into the piston and check the play between them. The piston pin hole worn from the rubbing will induce abnormal noises.

    If the rubbing resistance between the piston pin and the needle bearing on the connecting rod smaller end is too great, piston pin hole may be worn off. If you find, wear in the pin hole, change the piston with a new one and check the small-end bearing, too.

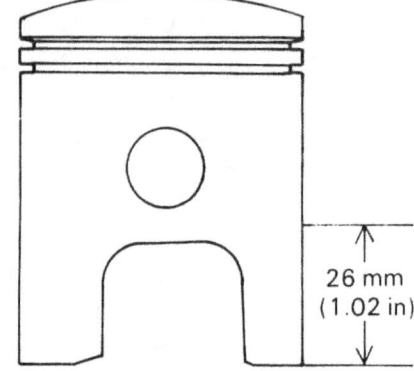

Fig. 6-6-1 Point to be measured

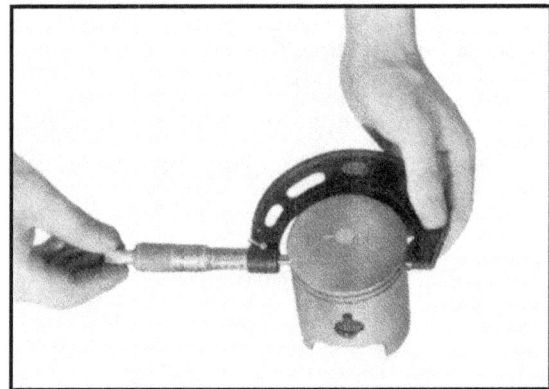

Fig. 6-6-2 Measuring piston diameter

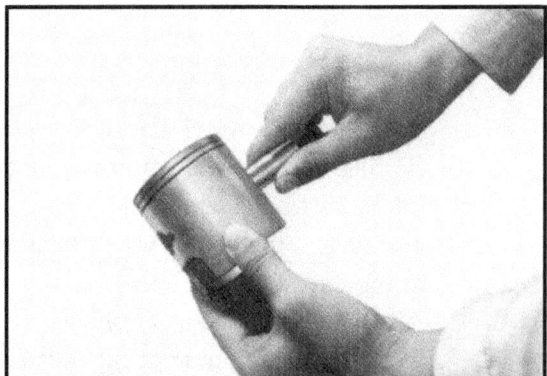

Fig. 6-6-3 Inspecting piston pin holes

3) Checking and repairing defects

Once the piston is subjected to seizure with seized mark left, it will reduce the engine power and the seizure tends to be repeated at the same part. So if you see a seizure mark, polish it away, using #400 waterproof abrasive paper. When the mark is too deep to be eliminated, replace the piston. (If there is a seizure mark on the piston a similar mark must be left on the cylinder wall. Repair the cylinder, too, with the #400 waterproof abrasive paper.)

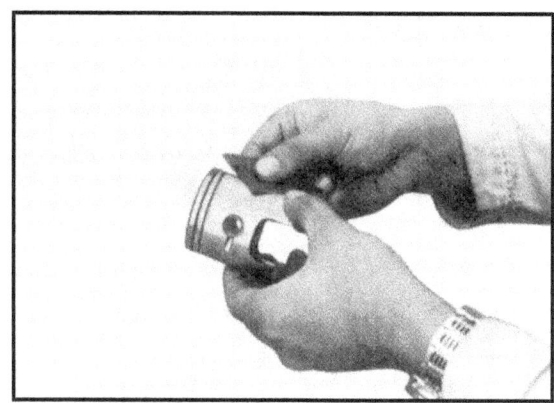

Fig. 6-6-4 Polishing piston surface

4) Removing carbon

Carbon deposited on the piston head tends to raise the compression ratio, prevent the effective cooling of the piston leading to advanced ignitions. Also, rings are stuck to the piston due to carbons deposited on the piston ring grooves. Therefore, such carbon deposits must be removed. The scrapped piston rings may be most conveniently used for cleaning the ring grooves.

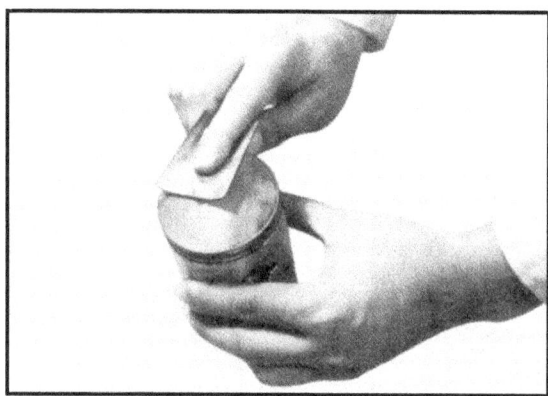

Fig. 6-6-5 Removing carbon

2. Caution in installing piston

1) In installing piston into cylinder, check if the arrow on cylinder is correctly aligned with the exhaust port side (front) of the cylinder.

2) Before installing the piston into the cylinder, make sure that the piston ring ends are aligned with the piston ring knock pin.

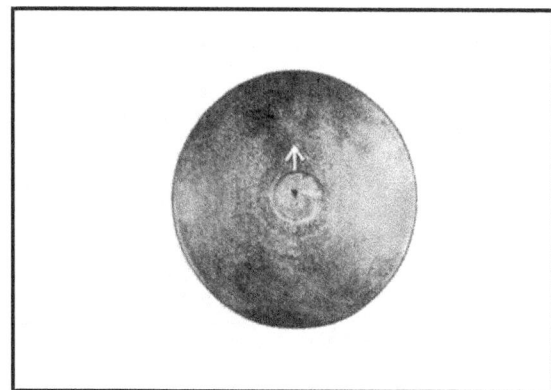

Fig. 6-6-6 Arrow mark

6-7. Oil pump

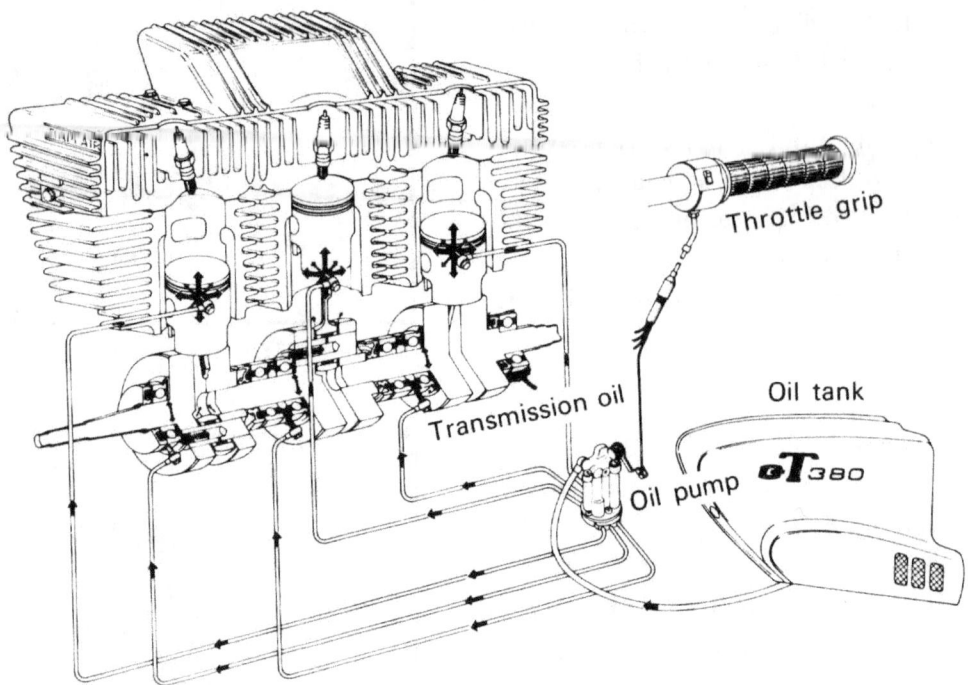

Fig. 6-7-1 Suzuki CCI system

The lubrication system for this engine uses "Suzuki C.C.I." system, which has been widely used in every model of SUZUKI and has its excellent lubrication performance and durability well established. The oil pump used for GT380 is the newly developed 6 outlet type, lubricating three crankshaft bearings and cylinders, respectively.

The oil pump is driven by the primary drive gear → primary driven gear → kick starter driven gear → kick starter idle gear → kick starter drive gear → oil pump drive shaft gear → oil pump drive shaft → oil pump driven gear. The reduction ratio between the crankshaft and the oil pump is 72.24 : 1.

1. Checking and adjuster

    The inner construction of oil pump is very intricate so that an overhaul will often offset the prescribed discharging amount leading to engine troubles. So never overhaul the oil pump. If the oil pump is found to be defective, replace it with a new one.

    In case any trouble has been found in the oil discharge rate, check all the parts relative to the pump and confirm the discharging rate again.

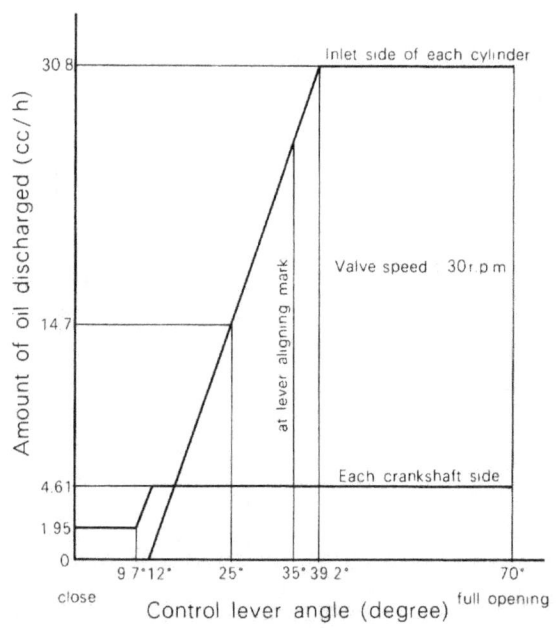

Fig. 6-7-2 Oil pump performance curves

1) Measuring discharging rate

   Measure the discharging amount in the following order after warming up the engine sufficiently.
   a. Set the measuring apparatus at the oil pump inlet.
   b. Run the engine at $2,000 \pm 100$ rpm.
   c. Raise the oil pump lever all the way to full open and start measurement.
   d. If the reading of decreasing amount of oil in the measuring apparatus is 2.82 - 3.74 cc after two minutes of measurement, there is no problem with the discharging rate of the oil pump.

   Note: Because the discharging rate varies with the engine speed keep the engine speed constant, using an accurate tachometer before starting the measurement.

2) Adjusting oil pump control cable

   The control cable can be adjusted as follows. Loosen off the bolt of the alignment holes of the carburetor mixing chamber, move up the throttle valve until the upper part of alignment mark on the side of the throttlevalve comes upto the top part of alignment hole, and then use the cable adjuster to make the alignment markings on the oilpump and the oil pump control lever match (see Fig. 6-7-4).

Fig. 6-7-3 Throttle valve dent mark

Fig. 6-7-4 Oil pump lever aligning mark

3) Bleeding
   a. If air is present in the oil line from the oil tank to the oil pump, loosen the oil pump bleeder screw as shown in Fig. 6-7-5, and bleed until all air has been expelled from the oil.
   b. To expel air contained at the discharge side of the oil pump, remove the oil pump, and using oil filler, send in oil until all air has been expelled, then install the oil pump. For this purpose, be sure to use CCI oil or engine oil recommended by Suzuki.

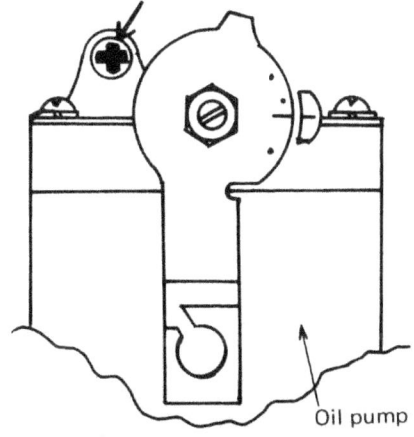

Fig. 6-7-5 Air bleeding screw

2. Tightening union bolt

   Tighten the union bolt to specified torques.

   The union bolt or the union bolt gasket will be damaged if tightened above the specified torque. Before fixing the bolts, check if the union bolt and gasket are defective or not.

   Union bolt tightening torque: 25 kg-cm (1.8 lb-ft)

6-8. Removing alternator

1. Remove the alternator cover

2. Separate the neutral switch lead wire from the neutral switch.

3. Loosen the three stator set screws.

4. Hold the small end of the left connecting rod with the piston holder and unfasten the rotor set bolt.

5. Fix the smaller end of the left connecting rod with piston holder and remove the rotor using rotor remover.

Fig. 6-8-1 Removing rotor

Note:

1. In mounting or dismounting stator, lift carbon brush off the slip ring by hand while you take off or fit the stator (This only applies to the Nippon Denso alternator.).

2. Before installing the alternator, make sure that there is no foreign materials sticking to the inner surfaces of rotor and stator.

3. The rotor remover comes in two kinds having different lengths. A screw with 60mm (2.36in) length of unthreaded part should be used for the Nippon Denso rotor, the one with 45mm (1.77in) for the Kokusan Denki rotor.

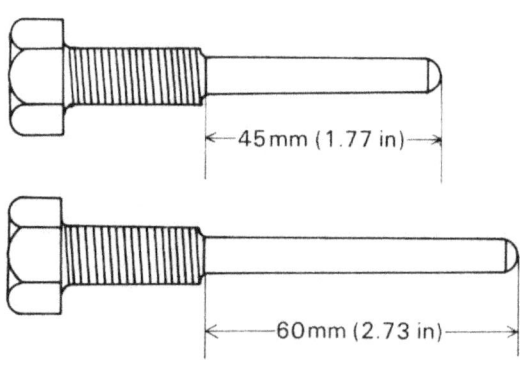

Fig. 6-8-2 Rotor remover

6-9. Contact breaker

1. Removal

   1) Remove the contact breaker inspection cap.

   2) Loosen the three breaker plate setting screws and remove the breaker from the crank case right cover.

2. Caution in installation

   1) Breaker lead wire must be led out of the case through A on the left side of the breaker fixing boss.

   2) After fixing with grommet, pull out the lead wire so that there is no play of wires inside the case.

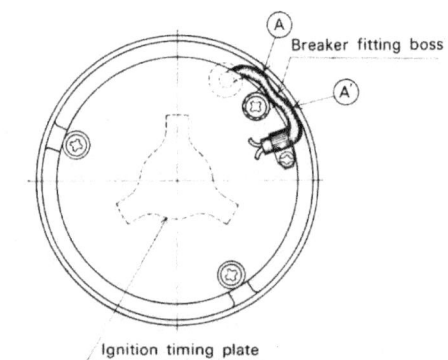

Fig. 6-9-1

3) In case the lead wire is led into the reverse side of the breaker plate through A' on the right side of the breaker fixing boss, the timing plate may come in contact with the lead wire and eventually may cut it off.
So the rules 1) and 2) of above must be strictly observed.

* The adjustment of ignition timing will be discussed in the chapter of "Engine Electrical Equipment"

6–10. Servicing of contact breaker cam shaft

In case it becomes necessary to loosen the breaker cam fitting nut because of unexpected trouble of the ignition timing plate and the breaker cam, be sure to dismount the right crank case cover first and then loosen the nut. Do not loosen the breaker cam fitting nut with the right crank case cover being in home position, or the cam shaft driven gear made of nylon will be broken.

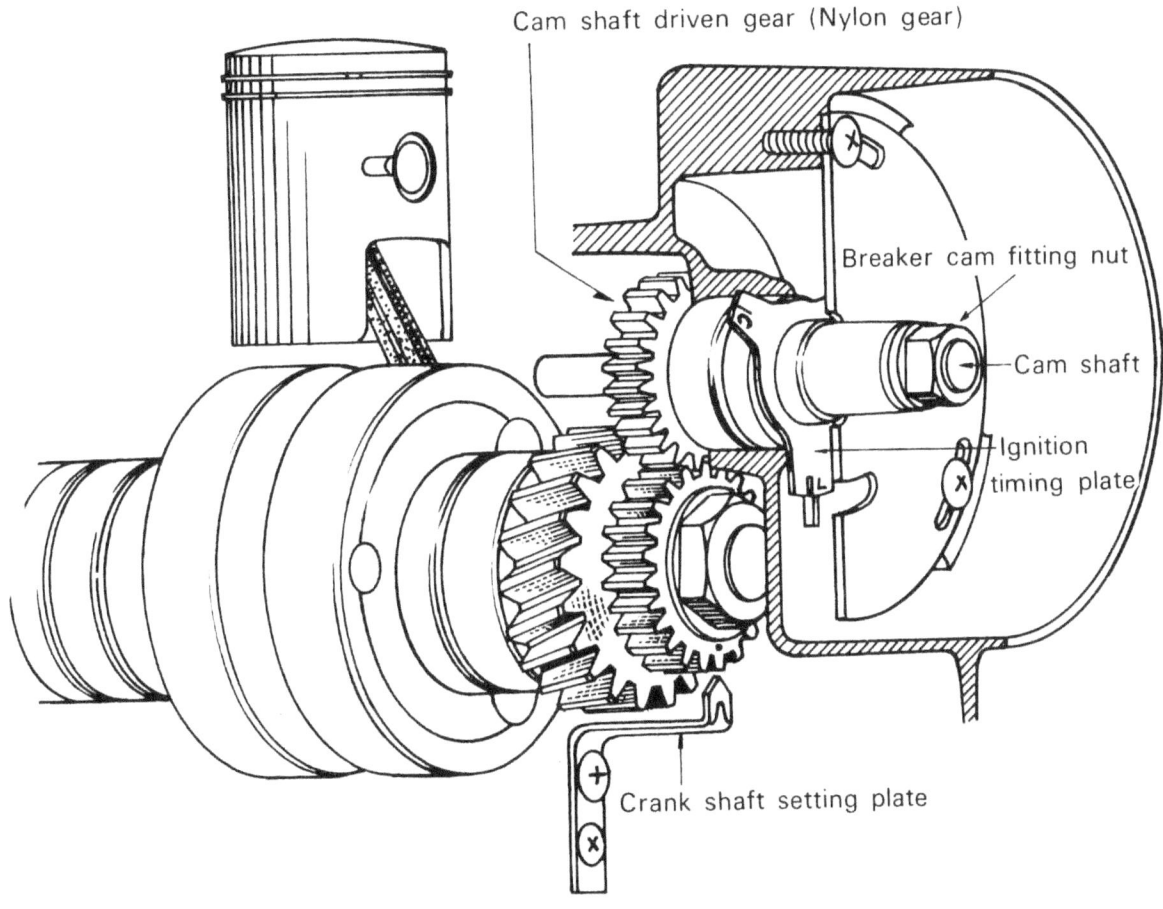

Fig. 6–10–1

6–11. Right crank case cover

Since the driving of the contact breaker cam of this engine is done through the breaker cam shaft drive gear and the cam shaft driven gear is made of nylon, special attention should be paid in dismounting and mounting the right crank case cover.

Not following the correct procedure will possibly cause breakage of the gear.

1. Removing
    1) Loosen the kick starter lever set bolt and take off the kick starter lever.
    2) Loosen nine crank case right cover screws and remove the crank case right cover. As the two screws locate inside the contact breaker plate, they should be unscrewed after removing the contact breaker plate. But when you take off the cover, confirm that the cover gasket does not stick to the cover. In case it is stuck to the cover, peel it off using a knife or the equivalent before removing the cover.

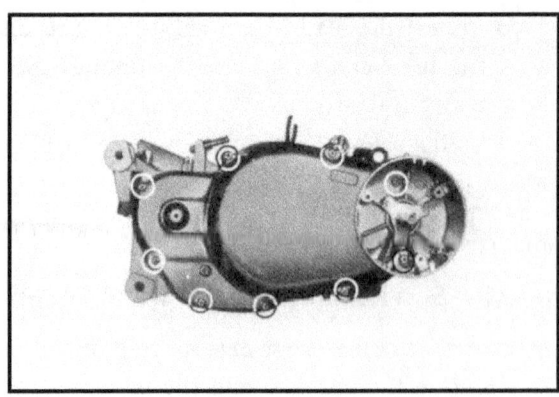

Fig. 6–11–1 Crank case right cover fitting screws

    3) Remove the crank case right cover gasket. Then check visually if the gasket is still usable.
    (As a rule, however, the gasket must be replaced when you disassemble and assemble the engine.)

    Caution: When you take off the crank case right cover, do not loosen the contact breaker cam fitting nut, for it is not necessary to remove the contact breaker cam, cam shaft and ignition timing plate.

2. Installing
    Since the contact breaker cam and cam shaft are assembled with the crank case right cover, the following procedure must be observed when you reset the crank case right cover.
    1) Align the punched mark on the breaker camshaft drive gear fitted on the crank shaft with the alignment mark on the crank shaft setting plat (see Fig. 6-11-2).
    2) Align the dented mark (red line) of the L mark on the ignition timing plate attached to the cam shaft with the alignment mark on the crank case right cover (see Fig. 6-11-3).
    3) After performing 1) and 2), match the knock pin of the crank case with the pin hole of the crank case right cover and set the cover.

    Caution: Unless the above works properly carried out, the proper ignition timing will never be obtained.

Fig. 6–11–2

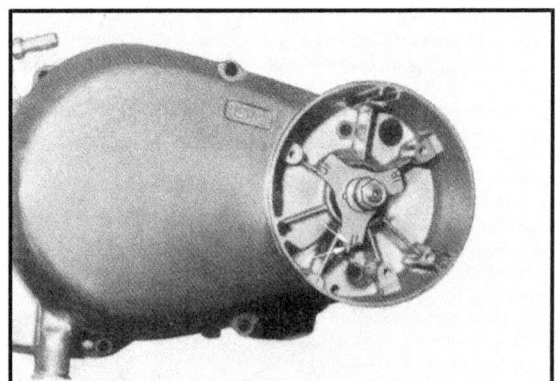

Fig. 6–11–3

6-12. Clutch

The function of the clutch is to transmit or disengage the power produced by the engine for the driving of the rear wheel through the transmission gears. Fig. 6-12-1B is a schematic drawing of the operating principles of the wet type, multiple palte clutch equipped on GT380.

The drive plates are turned by the clutch housing rotating in accordance with the engine revolutions. The driven plates are meshed in the sleeve hub on the countershaft, and are unable to transmit power in this state. But when pressed together between the drive plates by the force of the clutch spring acting through the pressure plate, the frictional force produced allows power to be transmitted.

When the clutch is disengaged, the spring force acting on the pressure plate does not act on the clutch plates. Therefore, the frictional force is decreased and the transmission of power between the plates is cut off.

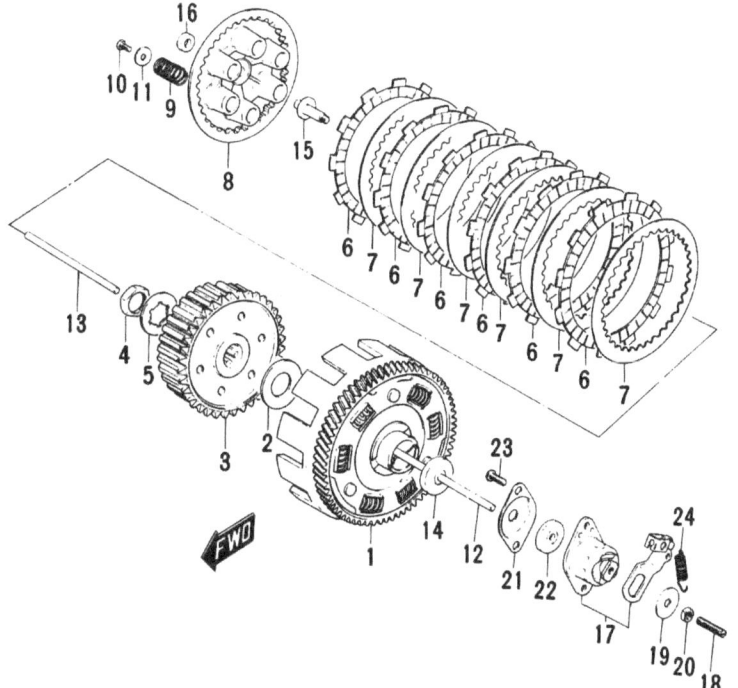

1	GEAR ASSY, primary driven	1	NT:68
2	THRUST WASHER, clutch sleeve hub	1	20x44x3
3	HUB, clutch sleeve	1	
4	NUT, clutch sleeve hub	1	
5	WASHER, clutch sleeve hub	1	
6	PLATE, cork	6	
7	PLATE, clutch driven	6	
8	DISK, clutch pressure	1	
9	SPRING, clutch	6	
10	BOLT	6	
11	WASHER, clutch spring	6	6.5x20x1.6
12	ROD, clutch push (1)	1	L:123, D:6
13	ROD, clutch push (2)	1	L:177, D:6
14	OIL SEAL, clutch push rod	1	4.5x30x7
15	PIECE, clutch push	1	
16	OIL SEAL, clutch push piece	1	10x17x5
17	SCREW ASSY, clutch release	1	
18	SCREW, clutch release adjusting	1	
19	WASHER, clutch release screw	1	6.5x24x1.2
20	NUT	1	
21	COVER, clutch release screw	1	
22	DUST SEAL, clutch release screw	1	
23	SCREW	2	
24	SPRING, clutch release return	1	

Fig. 6-12-1A

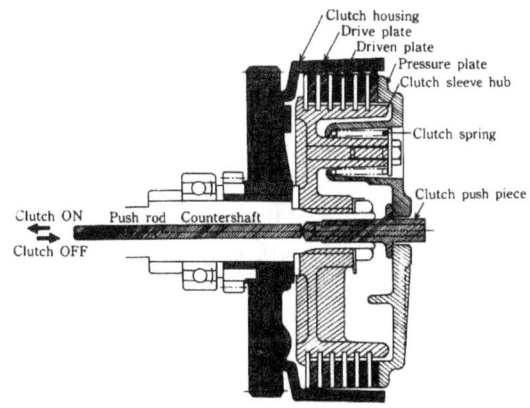

Fig. 6-12-1B

1. Clutch cushioning device

   For the purpose of performing smoother transmission when engaging or disengaging the power from the engine, the primary driven gear has been assembled to the clutch housing with cushioning matter placed in between. In the GT380 clutch, two varieties of coil springs have been employed in order to ensure sufficient cushioning for quick transmission of high power.

2. Primary reduction ratio

   No. of teeth in primary drive gear 24
   No. of teeth in primary driven gear 68
   Primary reduction ratio . . . . 68/24 . . . . . 2.833

3. Disassembling

   1) Remove the clutch spring fitting bolts on clutch pressure plate with 10-mm wrench.
   2) Remove the pressure plate, release rod, drive plates, and driven plates from the clutch housing.
   3) Pry up bent lock tongue of clutch sleeve hub washer with a chisel. Using clutch sleeve hub holder (special tool 09920-51510), secure the clutch sleeve hub and loosen the clutch sleeve hub nut with 27 mm socket wrench.
   4) Remove the clutch sleeve hub and clutch housing from the countershaft.

Fig. 6-12-2 Loosening clutch sleeve hub nut

4. Inspecting clutch parts

   Improper use of the clutch, incorrect adjustments, or use of low grade transmission oil may result in excessive wear of the clutch parts. In such case, abnormal noise will be produced, or clutch slipping may develop, leading to insufficient transmission of power. Therefore, when the clutch is disassembled, the parts should be inspected carefully and any defective part found should be replaced.

   1) Clutch drive plates

      Inspect the clutch drive plates to see if the surfaces are burnt or roughened, and measure the thickness and warpage (run-out) to see if within the specified limits. Replace if found defective.

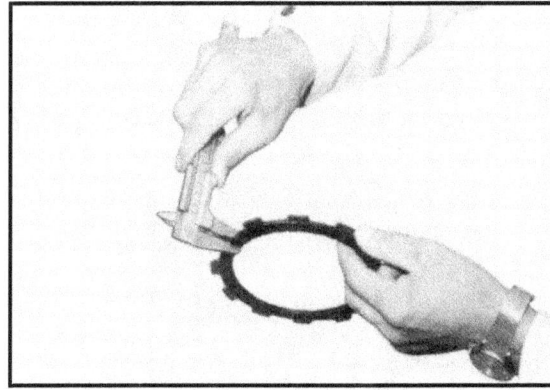

Fig. 6-12-3 Measuring drive plate thickness

	Standard	Limit
Thickness	3.5mm (0.138 in)	3.2mm (0.126 in)
Warpage	Under 0.4mm (0.016 in)	0.4mm (0.016 in)

2) Clutch springs

   If the clutch spring free length should become 1.5 mm or more shorter than the standard, there will be possibility of slipping clutch.
   Spring free length 38.4 mm (1.15 in).

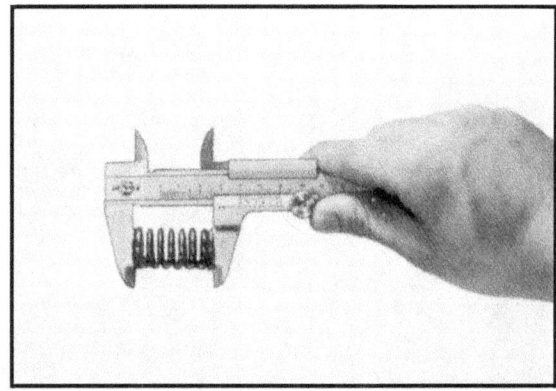

Fig. 6-12-4 Measuring clutch spring free length

3) Clutch housing

Inspect the primary driven gear tooth surfaces for abnormal conditons. check the axial play between primary driven gear and housing. Check the radial play between clutch housing and countershaft.

4) Clutch sleeve hub

If there are dented wear in the clutch sleeve hub splines, the clutch driven plates may stick when the clutch is disengaged and result in the clutch to lose smoothness of operation.

Repair or if the wear is excessive, replace with new part.

5) Clutch release screw

Check for excessive looseness by moving the release screw arm back and forth. If excessively loose, cracked, or injured, the clutch will not operate smoothly so in such case, replace the entire release screw assembly.

6) Clutch push rods

Pull out the two clutch push rods from the countershaft and check them for bending by rolling them on top of surface plate. A bent push rod will contact partially inside the countershaft during operation, resulting in eccentric wear, so that it should either be repaired or replaced.

5. Adjusting clutch

1) Adjusting clutch release screw.
   (a) Remove the engine sprocket outer cover.
   (b) Loosen the lock nut (A) with 12-mm box wrench.
   (c) Tighten the adjusting screw (B) until it contacts push rods inside release screw lightly, and then return the adjusting screw one-fourth turn. After checking the clutch lever to see that it has proper play, tighten the lock nut.

2) Adjusting clutch cable
   (a) Loosen the clutch cable adjusting lock nut. (a).
   (b) With the clutch cable adjuster (b), adjust so that there will be about 4 mm (0.16 in) play at the clutch lever and then tighten the lock nut.

Fig. 6-12-5 Adjusting clutch release screw

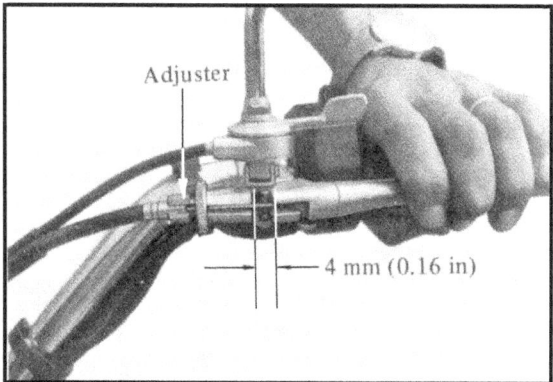

Fig. 6-12-6 Adjusting clutch lever

6–13. Primary pinion and breaker cam shaft drive gear

1. Removing
   1) Take off the crank shaft setting plate.
   2) Flatten the breaker cam shaft drive gear lock washer at the bend with a chisel.
   3) Hold the right hand connecting rod at the small end, using the piston holder (Special tool No. 09910-20113), and loosen the breaker cam shaft drive gear nut.
   4) Remove the breaker cam shaft drive gear, primary pinion and lock washer by hand.

2. Assembly
   Assembling must be done in the reverse order of the disassembling. When you fasten the breaker cam shaft drive gear nut, use the torque wrench to tighten it to specified torque.
   Tightening torque: 500 kg-cm (36 lb-ft)

6–14. Crank case

1. Disassembling crank case
   1) Remove the crank case fastening bolts (upper side 9 bolts. Lower side 18 bolts)
   2) Numbers are indicated on the crank case which show the tightening order of the bolts. So when you unfasten the bolts, start from the biggest number to the smaller, that is 27 . . . . . . 1.
   3) Disassemble the crank case, tapping it lightly with a plastic hammer.

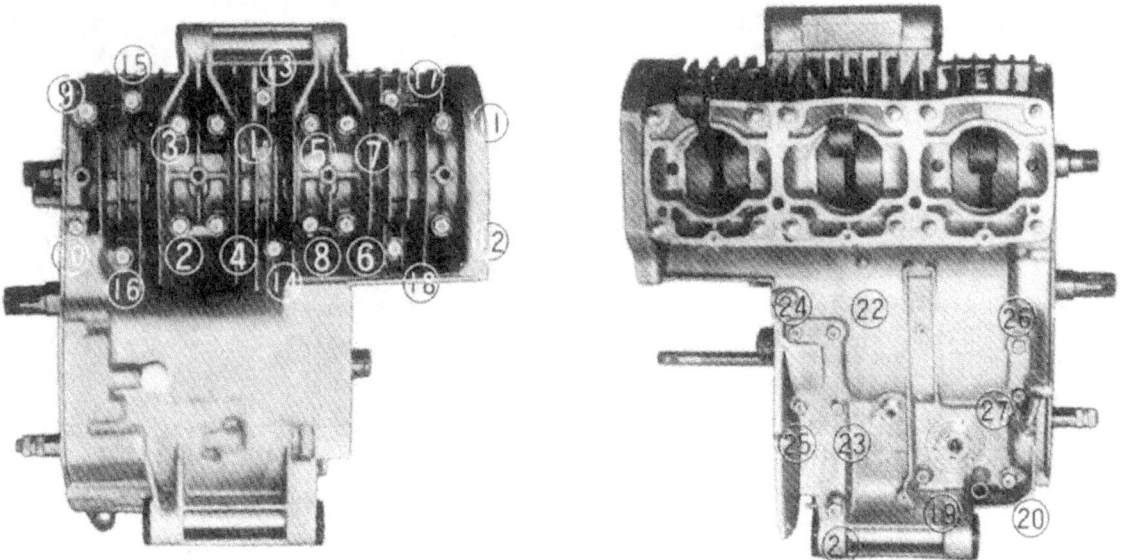

Fig. 6–14–1 Crank case set bolts tightening order

2. Assembling
   1) Clean the fitting surface of crank cases with benzine.
   2) Apply liquid gasket (parts No. 99000-31010) onto the upper crank case. But do not apply excessively, for the liquid gasket sometimes clog the lubricating oil passage of the right crank bearing.
   3) Fit the crank case properly and fasten the crank case fastening bolts. When you do this, first fasten the bolts provisionally, then tighten them to the specified torque in the order of the numbers marked on the crank case.

   Specified tightening torque
         6mm bolts . . . . 130 kg-cm (9.4 lb-ft)
         8mm bolts . . . . 200 kg-cm (14.5 lb-ft)

6−15. Transmission

Cautions of installing

1.) Wash all the gears and shafts clean before you install them.
2.) Before mounting the upper crank case, check if the gear shift functions properly and that there is no such abnormality as misattachment.
3.) When you put each gear and shaft to the lower crank case, make sure that each bearing is matched with the knock pin.
4.) After the upper crank case is attached, check if the drive shaft and counter shaft can be turned smoothly by hand. (Compared with other models, this may give you the impression that these shafts are somewhat heavy, but it does not mean any abnormality since GT380 employs the neutral brake.)

The relative positions of the gears and washers are as shown in Fig. 6-15-1.

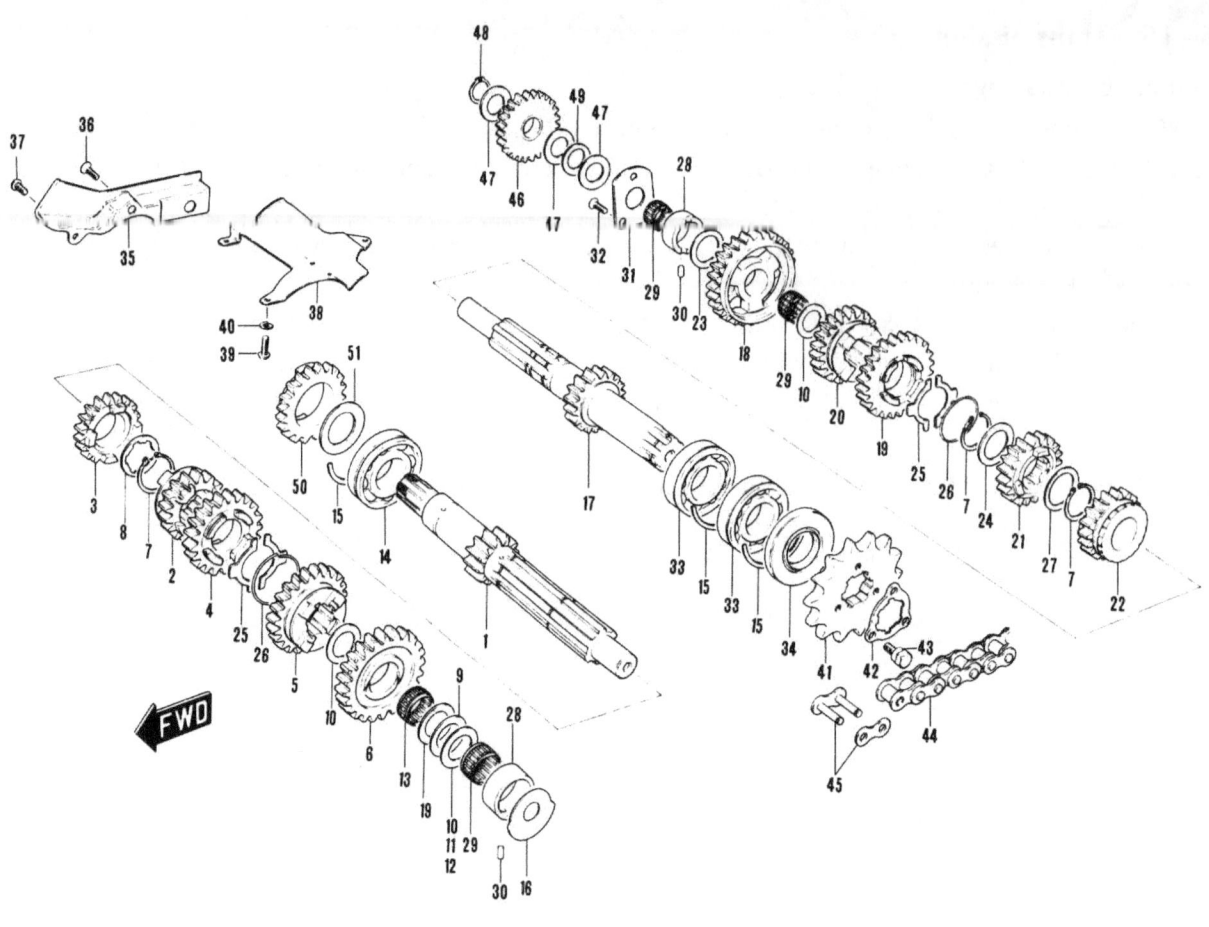

1	COUNTER SHAFT	1	NT:12		27	THRUST WASHER, 4th driven gear	1	
2	GEAR, 2nd drive	1	NT:16		28	BUSHING, transmission shaft	2	21x30x13
3	GEAR, 3rd drive	1	NT:19		29	BEARING, transmission shaft	3	17x21x12.8
4	GEAR, 4th drive	1	NT:21		30	PIN, transmission shaft bushing	2	
5	GEAR, 5th drive	1	NT:23		31	RETAINER, driveshaft	1	
6	GEAR, 6th drive	1	NT:24		32	SCREW, retainer	3	
7	CIRCLIP, 3rd drive gear	3			33	BEARING	2	
8	LOCK WASHER, 3rd drive gear	1			34	OIL SEAL, driveshaft	1	24.4x52x7
9	THRUST WASHER, 6th drive gear	1	17x29x1		35	CUP, oil reserver	1	
10	THRUST WASHER, 6th drive gear	2~4	17x29x1		36	SCREW	1	
11	THRUST WASHER, 6th drive gear	0~1	17x29x1		37	SCREW	1	
12	THRUST WASHER, 6th drive gear	0~2	17x29x1.2		38	PLATE, oil guide	1	
13	BEARING, 6th drive gear	1	17x21x9.8		39	SCREW, oil guide plate	3	
14	BEARING, counter shaft	1	25x52x15		40	LOCK WASHER	3	
15	C RING, counter shaft	3			41-1	SPROCKET, engine	1	NT:14, STD
16	RETAINER, counter shaft	1	NT:17		41-2	SPROCKET, engine	1	NT:16, OPT
17	DRIVESHAFT	1	NT:28		42	PLATE, engine sprocket	1	
18	GEAR, first driven	1	NT:24		43	BOLT, plate	3	
19	GEAR, 2nd driven	1	NT:27		44	CHAIN ASSY, drive	1	L:104
20	GEAR, 3rd driven	1	NT:22		45	JOINT, chain	1	OPT
21	GEAR, 4th driven	1	NT:19		46	GEAR, kick starter idle	1	NT:29
22	GEAR, 5th driven	1	NT:18		47	THRUST WASHER, kick idle gear	3	17x29x1
23	THRUST WASHER, 1st driven gear	1	17x28x3		48	CIRCLIP, idle gear	1	
24	WASHER, 4th driven gear RH	1	25x35x1.5		49	WAVE WASHER, idle gear	1	
25	RING, 2nd driven gear	4			50	GEAR, kick starter driven	1	NT:21
26	CIRCLIP, 2nd driven gear	2			51	WASHER, kick starter driven	1	25x41x3

Fig. 6-15-1 Exploded view transmission

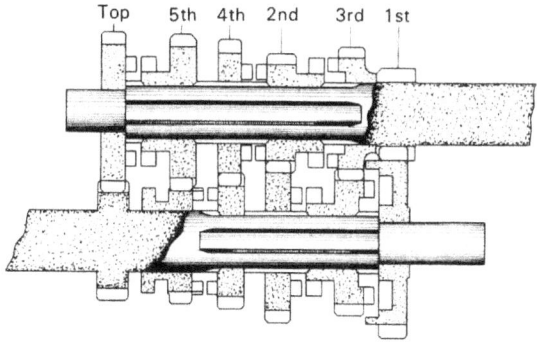

Fig. 6-15-2 Neutral position

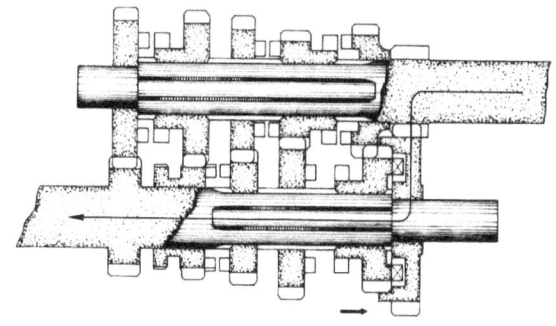

Fig. 6-15-3 1st position

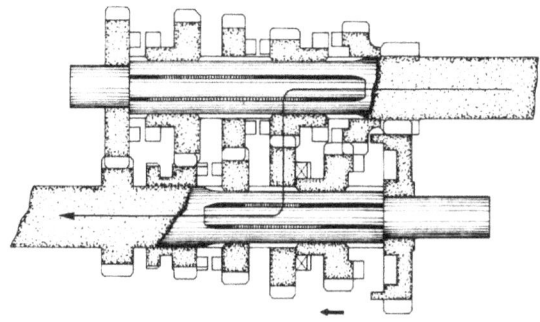

Fig. 6-15-4 2nd position

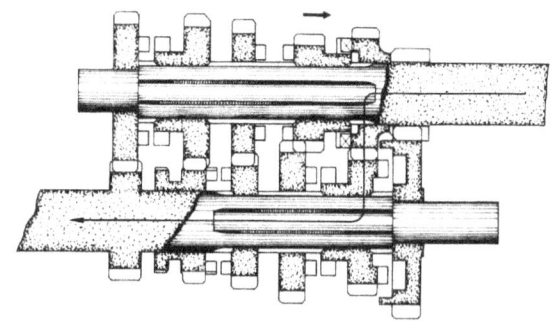

Fig. 6-15-5 3rd position

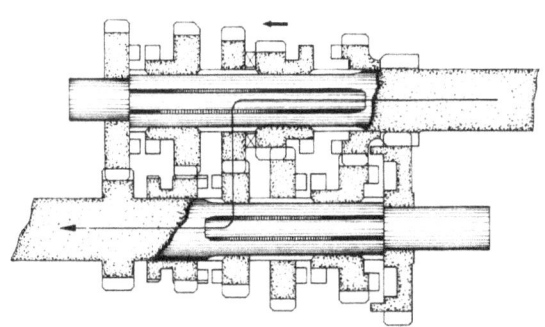

Fig. 6-15-6 4th position

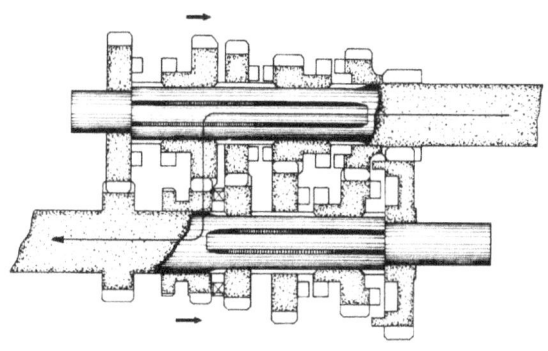

Fig. 6-15-7 5th positon

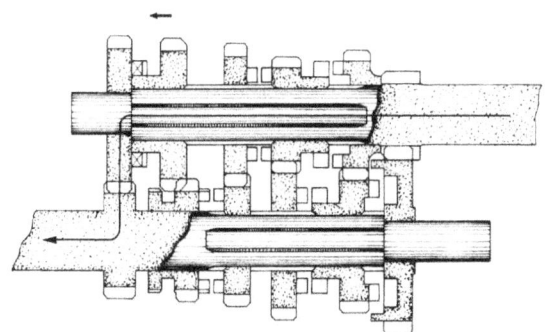

Fig. 6-15-8 Top position

6−16. Kick starter mechanism

This is a primary kick starter mechanism and differs from the conventional kick starter mechanism in that it does not operate through the clutch but turns the crankshaft directly through a gear train. As long as the clutch is disengaged, kick starting is possible regardless of the transmission gear position. The primary kick starter mechanism is illustrated in Fig. 6-16-1.

1. Operation

    Before kick starting, the ratchet wheel is held by the ratchet wheel guide. Upon kick starting, the kick starter shaft rotates in accordance with the kick lever. The ratchet wheel being in mesh with the kick starter shaft also starts to turn, and on releasing from the ratchet wheel guide, the ratchet wheel is pushed toward the kick drive gear by the force of ratchet wheel spring where it meshes against the side of kick drive gear. The kick drive gear through its related gears then turns the crankshaft.

    The transmission of power at kick starting takes place as follow :

    Kick Lever → Ratchet Wheel → Kick Drive Gear → Kick Idle Gear → Kick Driven Gear → Primary Driven Gear → Primary Pinion → Crankshaft

    On releasing the kick lever, the kick starter shaft is returned to its former position by the kick spring. At this time, the ratchet wheel which turns together with the kick starter shaft, due to the ratchet wheel guide, moves away from the kick drive gear.

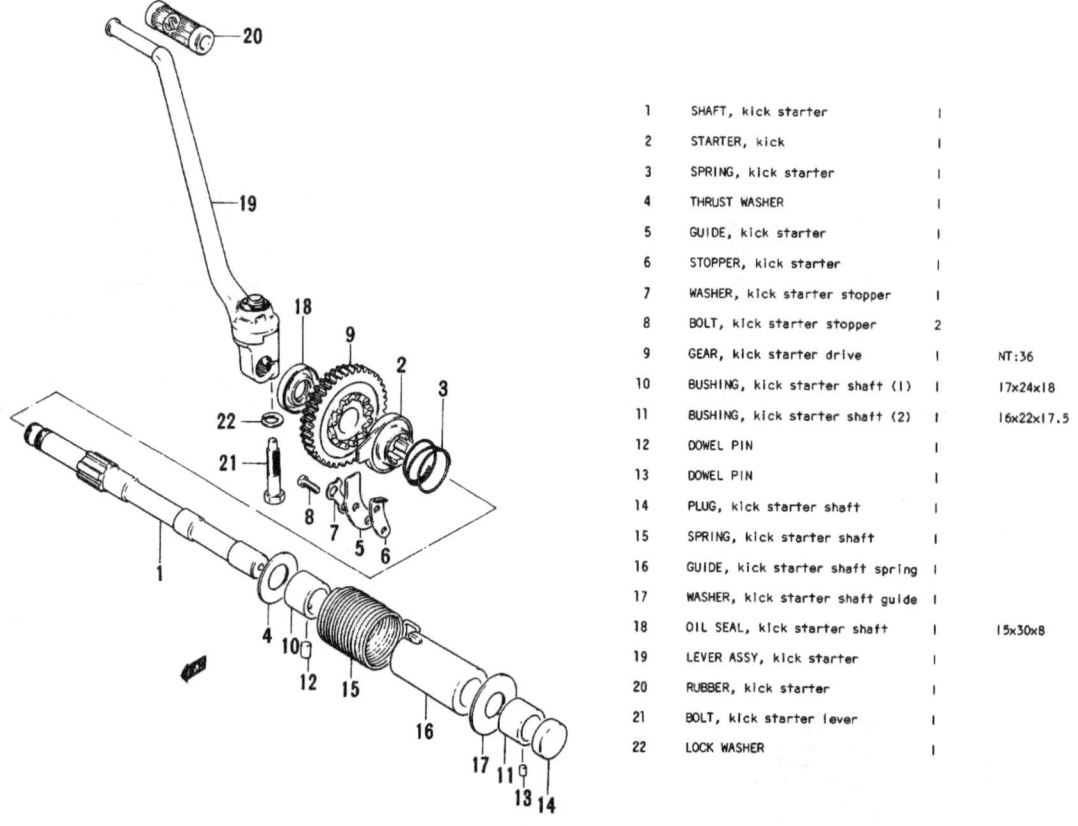

1	SHAFT, kick starter	1	
2	STARTER, kick	1	
3	SPRING, kick starter	1	
4	THRUST WASHER	1	
5	GUIDE, kick starter	1	
6	STOPPER, kick starter	1	
7	WASHER, kick starter stopper	1	
8	BOLT, kick starter stopper	2	
9	GEAR, kick starter drive	1	NT:36
10	BUSHING, kick starter shaft (1)	1	17x24x18
11	BUSHING, kick starter shaft (2)	1	16x22x17.5
12	DOWEL PIN	1	
13	DOWEL PIN	1	
14	PLUG, kick starter shaft	1	
15	SPRING, kick starter shaft	1	
16	GUIDE, kick starter shaft spring	1	
17	WASHER, kick starter shaft guide	1	
18	OIL SEAL, kick starter shaft	1	15x30x8
19	LEVER ASSY, kick starter	1	
20	RUBBER, kick starter	1	
21	BOLT, kick starter lever	1	
22	LOCK WASHER	1	

Fig. 6−16−1 Exploded view of kick starter

2. Precautions on reassembling
   1) Be sure to align the punch mark on the kick starter shaft with that on the ratchet wheel.
   2) After assembling the kick starter shaft in the crankcase, check the shaft to see that it turns easily.

6-17. Crankshaft

1. Cautions of mounting
   1) Apply Suzuki C.C.I. oil sufficiently to each bearing and connecting rod big end.

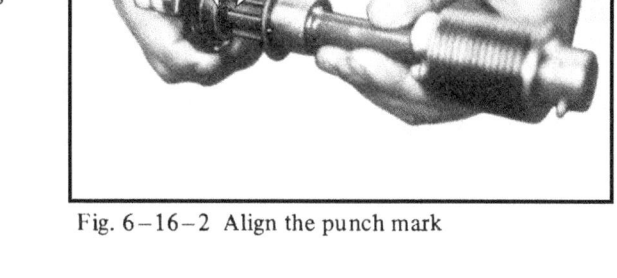

Fig. 6-16-2 Align the punch mark

   2) Each bearing has a pin which prevents the outer race from turning. Align the pin position to the dent on the fitting surface of crank case. If it is not well positioned, the crank case will be damaged.
   3) During the assembly, move each oil seal closer to the bearing so that it may not come in contact with the crank wheel.

6-18. Suzuki Recycle Injection System

Lubricating oil will accumulate in the crankcase during a continuous low-speed running on busy streets. During the rapid acceleration, the excess oil will be exhausted with exhaust gas through the muffler. In order to minimize this type of the phehomenon, this motorcycle adopts the system, whereby an excess lubricating oil in the crank case is led to the scavenging passage of the cylinder through an oil hose and is burnt completely in the combustion chamber. This reducing system of the exhaust gas (particularly during rapid accelerations) is called the Suzuki Recycle Injection System.

Fig. 6-18-1 shows the arrangement of the Suzuki recycle injection hoses.

Left crank case bottom → Center cylinder scavenging passage

Center crank case bottom → Right cylinder scavenging passage

Right crank case bottom → Left cylinder scavenging passage

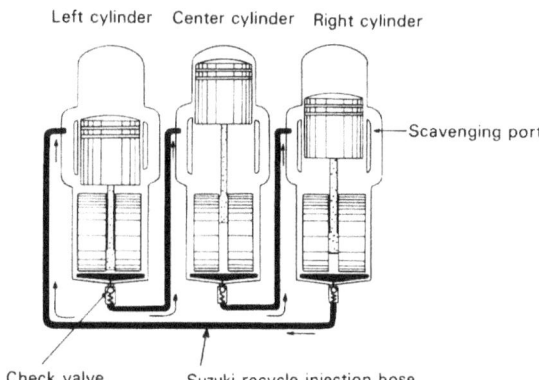

Fig. 6-18-1 Arrangement of the SRIS hoses

In case of any error in the arrangement, the system will not function properly, deteriorateing the engine performance. So be very careful. At the time of periodic checks (every 6,000 km (4,000 mi)), check the injection hoses to see if they many not be bardened due to the cylinder heat.

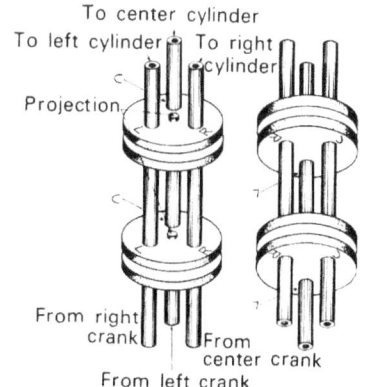

Fig. 6-18-2

1. Injection hose grommet
   The three injection hoses are led together through the back part between the left and the center cylinders. Both upper and lower crank cases use one grommet of the same type to position the

injection hoses. These grommets have the letters L, C and R indicating the positions of injection hoses. So attach them as shown in Fig. 6-18-2 (with the projection (ᵣ⊓ᵢ) at the center of the grommet side placed upper).

6-19. Oil seal

1. Removing oil seal

   In removing the oil seal, use the oil seal remover (special tool No. 09913-50110). Do not use screwdriver or similar tools as there is danger of damaging the oil seal lip.

2. Installing oil seal

   The oil seal can be installed easily by using oil seal installing tool.

   Notes:
   1) Before installing the oil seal, be sure to coat the oil seal lip with grease.
   2) Use care not to install the oil seal at an angle as this will allow the pressure to leak out. Coating the outer surface of the oil seal lightly with grease will enable installing the oil seal with greater ease.
   3) The general rule is to use new oil seals when reassembling the engine after overhaul.

Fig. 6-19-1 Applying grease

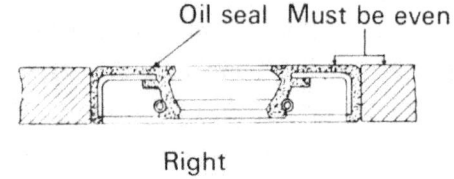

Right

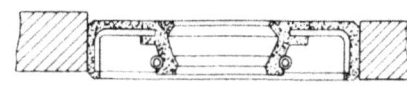

Wrong

Fig. 6-19-2 Fitting oil seal

6-20. Bearing

Inspecting bearing

Since the outer diameter of the bearing contracts slightly due to forcefitting allowance, a clearance is provided between the race and balls beforehand. Therefore, in inspecting the bearing for wear, judgement cannot be made by checking for excessive clearance. The only method is to spin the race and listen to the noise. If abnormal noise is heard while the race is being turned, the bearing is no good. Before starting inspection, wash the bearing in clean gasoline and then lubricate it. If the bearing is just washed and then spun, even a new bearing will give off abnormal noise due to lack of lubrication, and moreover, repeated spinning will damage the bearing. Therefore, care must be taken not to spin a dry bearing.

Fig. 6-20-1 Inspecting ball bearing

7. CARBURETOR

7-1. Specifications

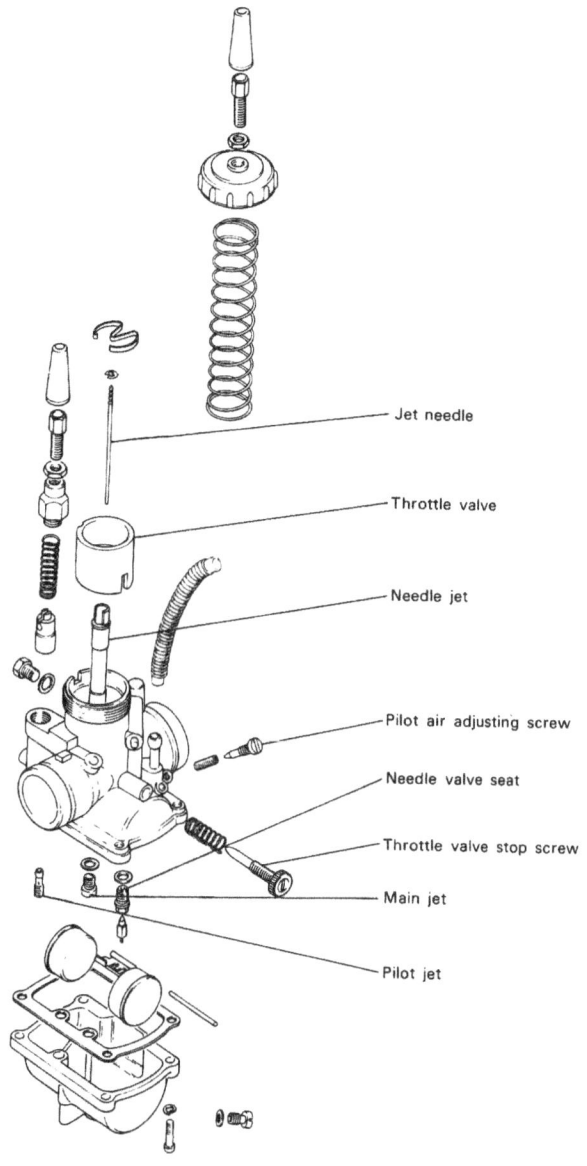

Type	VM24SC
Main jet	#80
Jet needle	4DH7-2
Needle jet	O-4
Throttle valve cut away	#3.0
Pilot jet	22.5
Pilot outlet	0.8
Pilot air adjusting screw	1¼ turns back
Needle valve seat	2.0
Float level	24.25 mm (0.955 in)

7-2. Overhauling carburetor

In overhauling the carburetor, remove all parts and after washing with clean gasoline, blow out the interior with compressed air. In cleaning out the jets, wire or other sharp objects must never be used as it will disturb the carburetor performance.

7-3. Adjusting carburetor

1. Adjust the throttle cable adjuster on each carburetor to obtain 3 - 5mm (0.1 - 0.2in) cable play.

2. Screw in the pilot air screw of each carburetor until it bottoms, then screw each one out 1¼ turns.

3. Start the engine and let it warm for about 5 minutes.

4. Adjust the idle speed according to the following system:

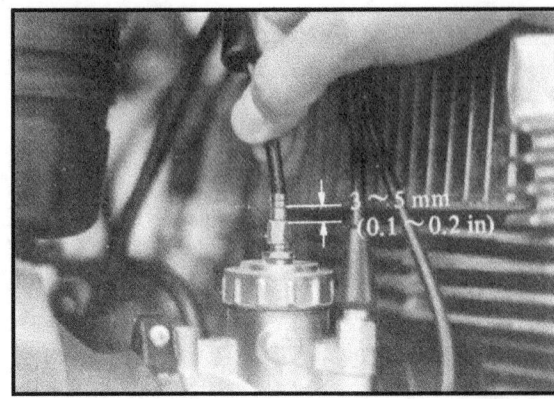

Fig. 7-3-1 Cable adjuster

⬜ L ⬜ = Left Cylinder

⬜ M ⬜ = Middle Cylinder

⬜ R ⬜ = Right Cylinder

 = Spark plug connected, cylinder running

⬜ = Spark plug disconnected, cylinder not running

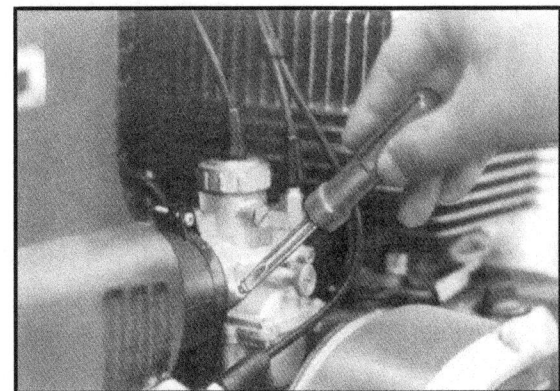

Fig. 7-3-2 Adjusting pilot air screw

1) Screw out each throttle stop screw 3½ turns from the bottomed position.
2) Start the engine and let it idle.

Fig. 7-3-3 Throttle stop screw

3) Remove the right spark plug cap and adjust the throttle stop screw on the M carburetor until 1,100 rpm reads on the tachometer.
4) Disconnect the middle spark plug cap and adjust the throttle stop screw on the R carburetor to 1,100 rpm.
5) Disconnect the left spark plug cap and read the idle rpm (X) with the M and R cylinders running.
6) Disconnect the right spark plug cap and adjust the throttle stop screw on the L carburetor to read X rpm obtained in step 5).
7) Repeat steps 4) and 5), and ascertain that X rpm is obtained in each case.
8) Connect all spark plug caps and screw out all throttle stop screws equally to bring engine idling speed to 1,100 rpm.

5. Synchronizing the carburetors:
In order to obtain maximum efficiency and throttle response, it is necessary that the throttle valve of each carburetor opens at the same time.
This can be adjusted as follows:
1) Remove the throttle valve inspection screws and twist the throttle grip until the throttle valve punch mark appears in this position.
2) Holding the throttle grip in that position, adjust each throttle cable adjusters so that each carburetor throttle valve is aligned at this postion as shown in Fig. 7-3-5.

Fig. 7–3–4 Throttle valve inspection screw

Correct　　　　　　　　　　　　　　　Incorrect
Fig. 7–3–5 Alignment of punch mark

3) Adjust final throttle cable play to 1 - 2mm at the handlebar cable adjuster.
4) This adjustment could affect the oil pump lever adjustment.
   Therefore, readjust the oil pump lever cable as necessary.

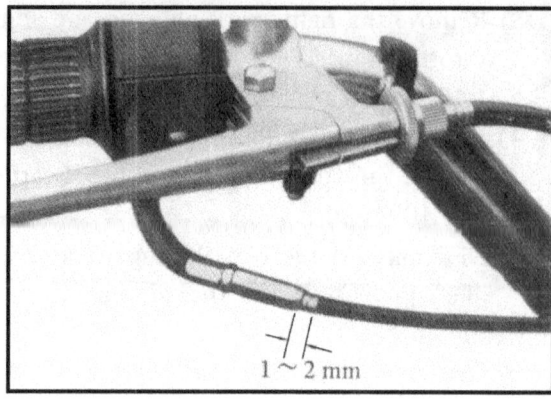

Fig.7-3-6 Throttle cable adjuster

7-4. Adjusting fuel level

1. Removing the float chamber body.
2. Turning up the mixing chamber.
3. As shown in Fig. 7-4-1, measure the height from the float chamber attaching surface to the float top.
4. Make adjustments to the height by bending the portion a (contacting area of needle vavle) in Fig. 7-4-2 so that the measured value of 3) will come within 24.25 ± 1mm.
   However, the float has to be replaced if it is indented or gasoline has leaked into it.
   Standard fuel level   24.25 ± 1mm (0.955 in)

Note: Because the fuel level is quite stable, there is usually no need of correction. But when the float was replaced with a new one or a marked abnormality occured in the carburetion, checking and adjustment must be exercised.

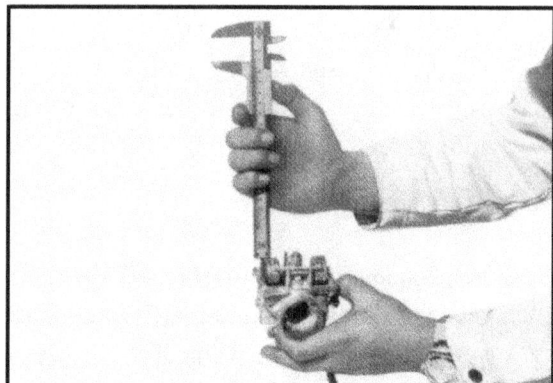

Fig.7-4-1 Checking fuel level

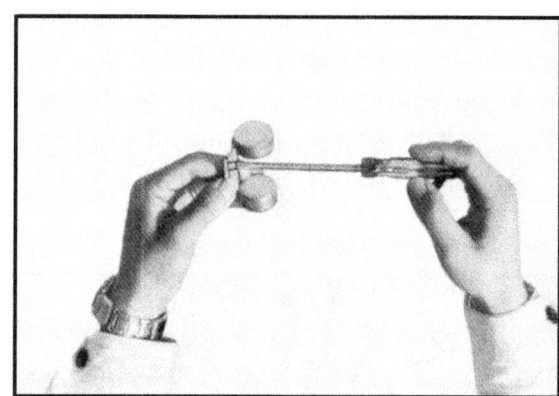

Fig.7-4-2 Adjusting float tongue

7-5. Inspecting float chamber parts

1. Float

   If gasoline should enter into the float while operating, the fuel level will become higher and will cause improper engine operation. Check the float by holding it in hand and seeing if there is any fuel inside. Replace if defective and also replace if deformed.

2. Needle valve

Inspect the needle valve visually to see if worn or damaged. If the defect cannot be detected visually hold carburetor mixing chamber body at the same level with its original position and turn it upside down with the needle valve installed and fuel pipe connected to the fuel tank. Allow the valve to close tightly on the valve seat by the weight of valve alone. Under this state, turn the fuel cock lever to "PRI" position and if there is no leakage of fuel, the valve is still usable.

3. Valve spring

If the spring inside the needle should become weakened, gasoline may overflow from float chamber when running at specified speed under specified road conditions. In case such condition arises, replace the needle valve.

7-6. Overflowing

If overflow still continues to develop even after making the checks directed in (7-5) above, there is a strong chance of dirt being caught between the needle valve and valve seat as shown in Fig. 7-6-1.

In such a case, close the fuel cock temporarily and run the engine so the fuel level inside the float chamber will drop. When the fuel level drops, the needle valve will drop correspondingly, causing the clearance between the valve seat and needle valve to grow larger. Under this state, reopening the fuel cock will allow the fuel to flow in through the valve seat with considerable force so that there is a good possibitlity

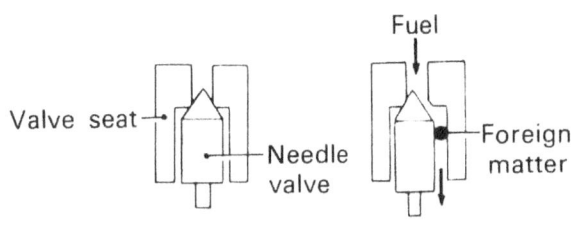

Fig. 7-6-1 Overflow caused by foregin matter

of the dirt stuck at this part being washed away and the trouble remedied. However, this is merely an emergency measure. If the overflow trouble is to be remedied basically, the dirt must be removed completely from the fuel. At this time, the filter in the fuel cock should also be inspected carefully. Since a large part of the overflow trouble is caused by adherence of dirt, if this trouble occurs too frequently, the fuel tank interior should be flushed out clean with gasoline. The users should also be advised to always close the fuel cock whenever the motorcycle is to be parked for any length of time.

7-7. Attaching carburetor

In mounting the cylinder, intake pipe and carburetor together as Fig. 7-7-1 shows, you can attach the carburetor straight up.

The attachment to the cylinder must be properly made in accordance with the indication marks on the starter side (Fig. 7-7-1) of the carburetor.

Left carburetor	Indication mark L
Center carburetor	" M
Right carburetor	" R

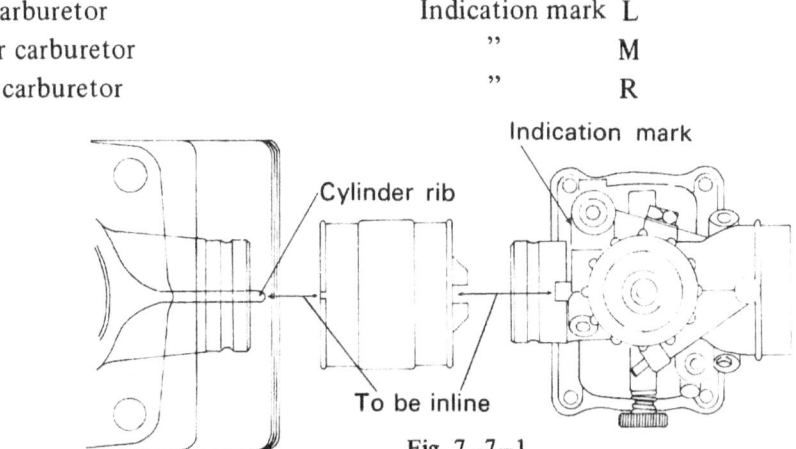

Fig. 7-7-1

8. ENGINE ELECTRICAL EQUIPMENT

8–1. Alternator

In order that the various electrical equipment can execute their functions with due consideration on "safety" the battery, their electrical source, must always be kept in the best possible condition. For this reason, we adopted, the alternator that demonstrates excellent charging performance even at the low-speed driving for this motorcycle.

1. Construction

    Electricity is supplied to the rotor with the field coil wound around through a brush. The armature-side coil is wound around the stator and so fixed. The generated electricity is rectified by six silicone diode, then used for charging the battery and then supplied to each load.

2. Features

    A normal DC dynamo has an armature on the rotor and field coil on the stator with the generated electricity being taken from the brush through commutator. Unlike the DC dynamo, the construction of alternator is opposite and therefore has the following features:-
    1) The rotor can be made smaller. (The field coil may be smaller than the generator coil.)
    2) The life of brush is semi-permanent. (Unlike the commutator contacting point of the brush is not rugged but rather perfectly flat, and the current flow within the field coil is less than that in the armature.)
    3) Since the armature is fixed. There is much less posibility of troubles such as disconnected wires, etc. (broken wire)

3. Charging circuit

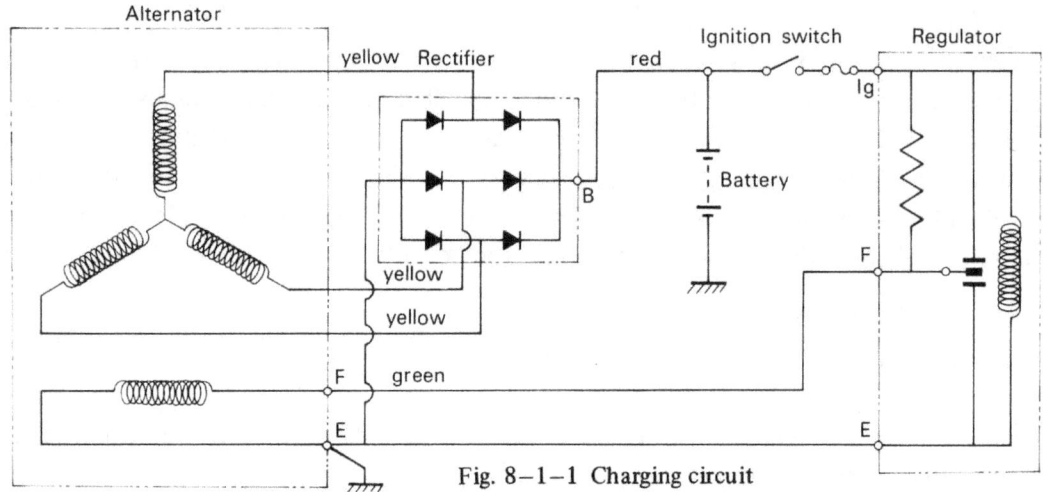

Fig. 8–1–1 Charging circuit

The charging circuit of the alternator is illustrated in Fig. 8-1-1. If the exciting current which flows in the rotor coil, remains constant, the voltage generated in the alternator stator coil is proportional to the number of rotations. As long as a battery is being charged, it is necessary to keep the voltage constant. And the role of regulator here is to reduce the exciting current whenever the generated voltage starts rising with the increasing rotational speed. Therefore, the principle of voltage regulation is based on the same principle as the conventional dynamo.

Turn on the ignition switch, and then the exciting current will flow from the battery. It first enters the regulator Ig terminal, goes through the point, leaving at the F terminal. Then it enters through the F terminal of the alternator and excites the rotor coil.

Now, as the engine starts, the rotor starts rotation inducing the three-phase alternating current in the stator coil. And the AC current will be rectified by the silicone rectifier and is charged into the battery through B terminal.

The terminal voltage of battery rises as the charging continues on, so will the voltage in the pressure-coil of regulator, and the contact point will be attracted. And the exciting current flowing in the rotor coil will decrease because it flows through a resistor, and thus the voltage generated in the alternator will be adjusted to regulated voltage.

Because the function of regulator used in alternator is only the adjustment of voltage, it requires neither cut-out relay nor current limiter. This is because the silicone rectifier prevents the reverse current from the battery (thus cut-out relay needs not be used) and the stator coil itself tends to keep the current under a certain level (thus avoiding the use of the current limiter).

4. Checking charging system

   1) Insulation test of stator coil

      Check if there is any conduction of electricity between each lead line from the stator coil and the body. The insulation is perfect if no electricity conduction is observed.

   2) Disconnection test of stator coil

      Check the conduction of electricity in each of the stator coil lead lines and all the measurements (at three points) must indicate being conductive. If not, some disconnection is most probable and the stator must be replaced.

	DENSO	KOKUSAN
Stator coil	0.26 - 0.1 Ω	0.43 - 0.1 Ω

   3) Disconnection test of rotor coil

      Check the conduction between two slip rings. If the conduction is not observed, replace the rotor complete.

	DENSO	KOKUSAN
Rotor coil resistance	10.5 - 11.5 Ω	4 - 5 Ω

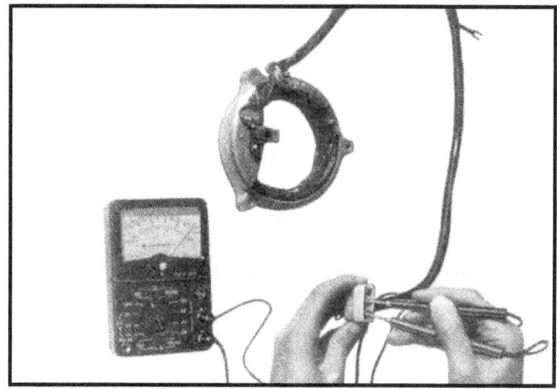

Fig. 8-1-2 Test of stator coil

   4) Checking brush

      The brush is semi-permanent. However, when the wear of 1/3 of the new brush dimension is observed, replace it. (Remove the brush holder, and set the brush spring free, and when the dimension of the brush outside of the brush holder is less than 7mm (0.28in), replace it with a new brush.)

      In the case of the KOKUSAN brush, replace it when the wear has progressed close to the wear limit mark.

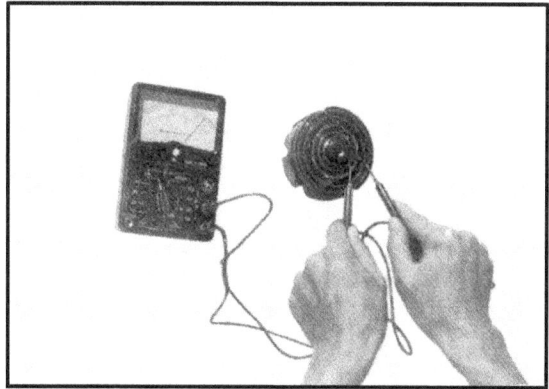

Fig. 8-1-3 Test of rotor coil

   5) Checking silicone rectifier

      Six silicone rectifiers are connected as illustrated in Fig. 8-1-4. Measure the resistance of each lead line and confirm that the measurements indicate very little resistance in the normal direction and infinitely large resistance in the reverse direction. Even if one of them is found to be defective, the whole rectifiers must be considered abnormal and need to be replaced.

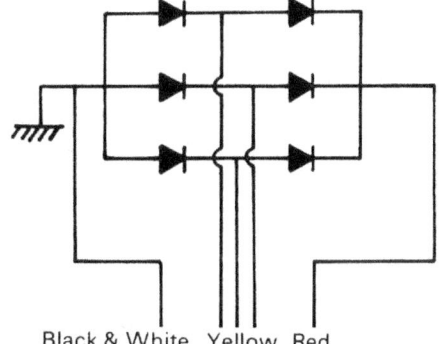

Black & White Yellow Red

Fig. 8-1-4 Silicon rectifier

6) Confirming the combined performance of alternator and silicone rectifier

The generating performance of the alternator must be measured with all the loads being eliminated. In Fig. 8-1-5, solid lines indicate the standard connection. Disconnect, the coupler at the regulator and connect the positive terminal of battery directly to the green wire. Remove the red wire connection (power line) from the coupler of the rectifier, and measure the voltage between this line and the earth (see dotted lines in Fig. 8-1-5). With all these accomplished, you can measure accurate voltage generated in the alternator, for it is now excited by the battery electrical sourse and all the loads have been eliminated. If the result of measurement is short of the values given below, there is some trouble in the alternator. Also even if it meets required values in case over discharge of battery is observed the source of trouble in other parts such as battery itself or silicone rectifire etc. may be located.

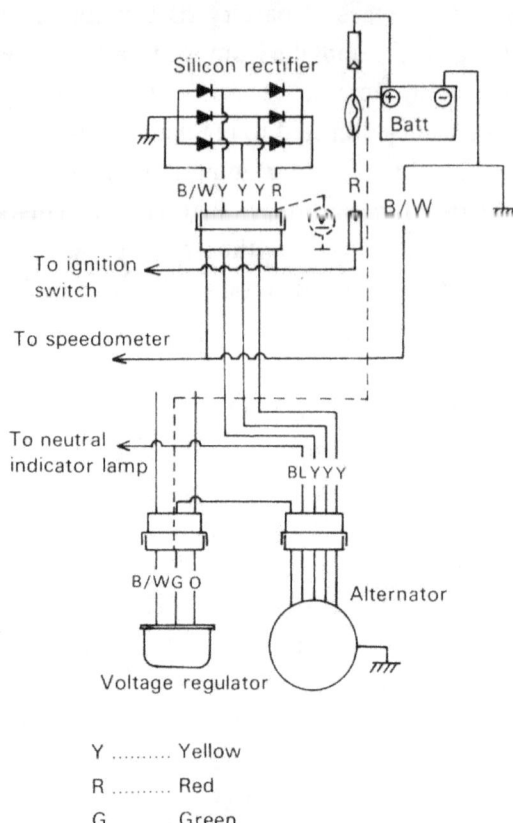

Y .... Yellow
R .... Red
G .... Green
O .... Orange
BL .... Blue
B/W ..... Black with White tracer

Fig. 8-1-5

Caution:
a. The time taken for the measurement must be as short as possible.
b. When you have to suspend the measurement, be sure to cut off the connection between the battery positive terminal and the rotor coil. This is needed to save the field coil from burning.

		DENSO	KOKUSAN
Minimum voltage to be generated	1,500 rpm	18V	22V
″ ″ ″	2,500 rpm	31V	40V

7) Checking regulated voltage

Measure the regulated voltage (voltage on charging circuit including the battery). Adjustment of regulated voltage can be made with the regulating arm (DENSO) or the regulating screw (KOKUSAN).

Regulated voltage   13.5 V - 14.5 V

8) Interchangeability of parts in charging system

Parts of both DENSO and KOKUSAN are used in the charging system of GT380. Therefore, when you replace parts, you should pay particular attention to the interchangeability between them.
(The silicone rectifier is the product of STANLEY).

a. Alternator & Breaker

The whole sets of DENSO and KOKUSAN parts may be interchanged at the time of assembly, however, a component part (brush, rotor, stator, breaker, cam, etc.) itself can not be interchanged.

b. Voltage regulator

DENSO and KOKUSAN regulators can be interchanged.

8-2. Ignition system

The ignition system employs a 3-contact points 3-ignition coils method with the battery as its electric source.

Three contact points are attached at an angle of 120° to each other.

The center contact point is different in form from remaining right and left hand contact, points.

These breaker assembly is attached on the crank case right cover. The crankshaft does not directly drive the camshaft, but by means of a gear in order to prevent the shaking of the camshaft. Thus the rotation of camshaft is opposite to that of crankshaft. Therefore, you ought to be careful when you adjust the ignition timing. (You may deal with this the same way as the adjustment of the conventional breakers set on the left side of the engine.)

Adjusting of ignition timing

The engine performance and the durability much depends on how the ignition timing its properly set and to what extent the timing for each cylinder is well balanced. It is, therefore, very important to set it precisely to specified proper position.

The ignition timing may be checked referring to marks on the ignition timing plate, however, the indication by this procedure may not be precise enough for the required timing. As a matter of fact, the designed purpose for this plate is to enable to know roughly and easily the relative position of the pistons to the contact point movement.

In this point of view, it is suggested not to use the alignment marks on the ignition timing plate when checking or adjusting the ignition timing as proper procedure, except for an emmergency purpose, but to use the ignition timing tester together with the ignition timing gauge (dial gauge) in the same manner as that for other models.

Contact point gap: 0.35mm (14/1,000 in)
Ignition timing: B.T.D.C. 3.0mm (allowance 2.52 - 3.76)
                     in piston stroke.

The ignition order is ① Left ② Center ③ Right.

8-3. Condenser capacity and ignition coil resistance

Condenser capacity   0.16 - 0.20 μF
Ignition coil resistance   primary coil   4 - 6 Ω
                           secondary coil   15 - 25 KΩ

9. BODY

9-1. Front fork

The following procedure should be followed at overhauling and repair.

1. Remove the front axle by loosening the axle holder at the bottom part of a fork outer tube first.
2. After pulling out an inner circlip as shown in the Figure using circlip remover (special tool No. 09900-06103), an outer tube is removable by pulling the outer tube downward while the inner tube staying at body side.
3. Feed 210 cc (0.45/0.36 pt. US/Imp) of motor oil 10W/30 to each front fork leg after assembly.

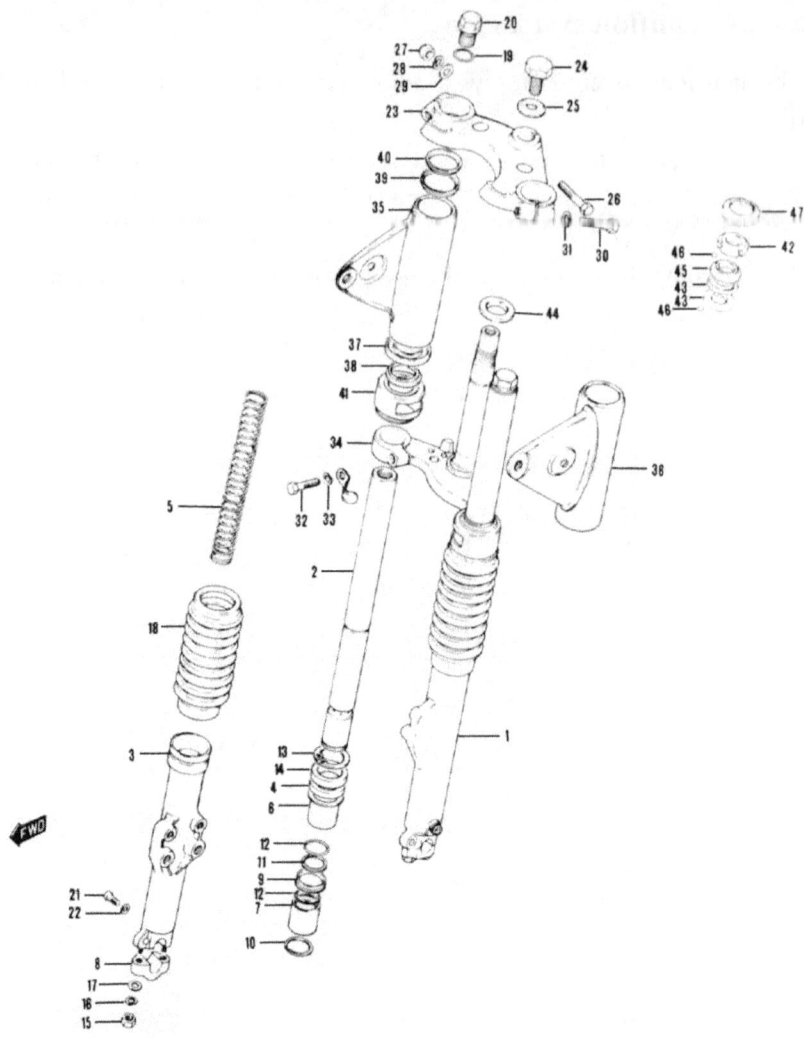

1	DAMPER ASSY, front fork	2	13	·CIRCLIP	2	25	WASHER, upper bracket	1	36-1	BRACKET, headlamp, LH	1
2	·TUBE, inner	2	14	·OIL SEAL	2		10.2×33×3.2		36-2	BRACKET, headlamp, LH	1
3	·TUBE, outer	2	15	·NUT	4	26	BOLT	1	37	SEAT, headlamp bracket	2
4	·OIL SEAL	2	16	·LOCK WASHER	4	27	NUT	1	38	CUSHION, headlamp bracket	2
5	·SPRING, fork	2	17	·LOCK WASHER	4	28	LOCK WASHER	1	39	CAP, headlamp bracket	2
6	·GUIDE, inner tube	2	18	·BOOT	2	29	WASHER	1	40	CUSHION, bracket upper	2
7	·PISTON, inner tube	2	19	·O RING	2	30	BOLT	2	41	GUIDE, boot	2
8	·HOLDER, axle	2	20	·CAP, inner tube	2	31	LOCK WASHER	2	42	NUT, steering stem	1
9	·VALVE, damper	2	21	·SCREW	2	32	BOLT	2	43	RACE, steering inner	2
10	·SNAP RING	2	22	·GASKET	2	33	LOCK WASHER	2	44	RACE, steering outer, upper	1
11	·RING, valve stopper	2	23	BRACKET, front fork upper	1	34	STEM, steering	1	45	RACE, steering outer, lower	1
12	·RING, piston stopper	4	24	BOLT, front fork upper bracket	1	35-1	BRACKET, headlamp, RH	1	46	BALL, steering steel	36
				D:10screw, L:20		35-2	BRACKET, headlamp, RH	1	47	DUST SEAL, steering upper	1

9-2. Brake

GT380 employs two leading brakes with the drum diameter of 180mm for the front wheel and the leading trailing brake with the drum diameter of 180mm for the rear wheel.

1. Checking and adjusting

    Fit brake shoes onto the brake panels and measure their outer diameters, closing the cam fully.

    Brake shoe wear limit

Outer diam. of brake shoe	Front wheel	Rear wheel
Wear limit	176mm	176mm

    Brake drum wear limit

Inner diam. of brake drum	Front wheel	Rear wheel
Wear limit	180.7mm	180.7mm

Adjusting front brake cam lever connecting rod
1) Loosen the lock nut of the connecting rod.
2) Turn the connecting rod toward the direction of ① as shown in the Fig. 9-2-1.
3) Pull the brake lever fully or push the brake cam first lever fully by hand.
4) Turn the connecting rod toward the direction of ② and the brake cam second lever will be drawn. When the brake shoes come in contact with the drum, the connecting rod will no longer rotate. So stop turning here.
5) Fasten the lock nut.

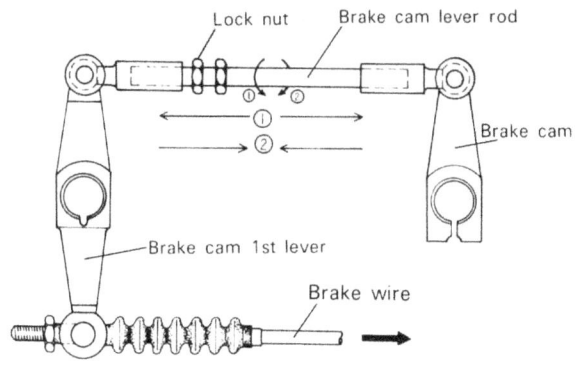

Fig. 9-2-1 Adjusting front brake cam lever connecting rod

Upon confirming all the above requirements are satisfied, adjust the brake wires:

Front brake .... Adjust the brake lever play so that the gap between the lever and the throttle grip becomes 20mm (0.8 in) when the brake is locked.

Rear brake .... Adjust the brake pedal travel so that the gap is 20 - 30mm (0.8 - 1.2in) when the brake is locked.

9-3. Drive chain

GT380 adopts a flaring type of joint for the drive chain from the strength point of view. Therefore, chain joint tool (special tool No. 09900-21802) must be used either to cut or joint the chain. The drive chain assembly and chain joint are available as replacement parts. Please note that new joint is definitely required once the chain is cut and never cut the same place twice.

Follow the instruction given with the tool when using chain joint tool.

Proper lubrication and adjustment of the drive chain prolong its service life and ensure smooth power transmission to the rear wheel. Poor maintenance will cause rapid wear or damage to the drive chain.

Fig. 9-3-1

Therefore, the drive chain must be checked and serviced after the first 800 km (500 miles) of operation and every 800 km (500 miles) thereafter, and lubrication is indispensable before the motorcycle is operated at sustained high speeds, or under conditions of frequent rapid acceleration.

—Inspecting and adjusting drive chain—

* Place the motorcycle on its center stand with transmission in neutral. Check the drive chain and sprockets for any of the following conditions:

Drive chain	Sprockets
○ Damaged Rollers	○ Excessively Worn Teeth
○ Loose Pins	○ Broken or Damaged Teeth
○ Dry or Rusted Links	○ Loosen sprockets nuts
○ Kinked or Binding Links	
○ Excessive Wear	
○ Improper adjustment	

* Measure the distance between a span of 20 pins, from pin center to pin center, with the chain held taut and any stiff joints straightened in order to determine if the chain is worn beyond its service limit. The distance of the new drive chain is 301.7 mm (11 7/8"), and if the distance exceeds 308.0 mm (12 1/8"), the chain is worn and must be replaced.

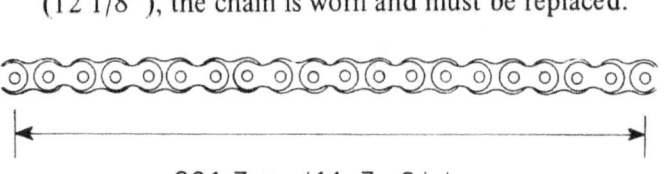

301.7mm (11 7/8 in)

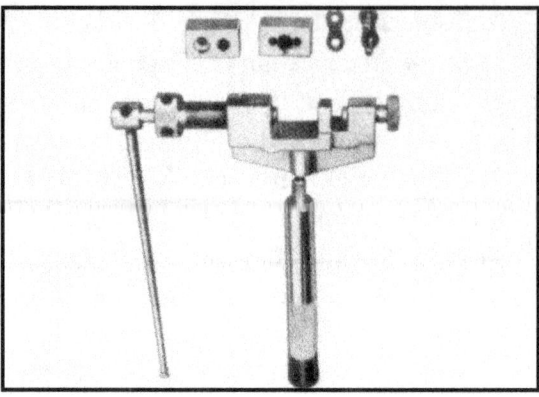

Fig. 9-3-2

* Check drive chain slack at the middle of the two sprockets by moving the chain up and down with fingers. Adjust the chain slack to 15–20 mm (0.6–0.8 in)

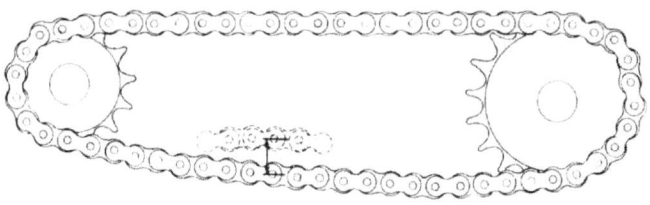

15–20mm (0.6–0.8 in)

9-4. Removing rear wheel

The rear axle bolt can not be removed to the side being blocked by four mufflers. Therefore, the rear wheel must be removed by the following procedure:

1. Pull out the cotter pin from the rear axle nut and loosen the nut.
2. Remove bolts, tightening the support to the tail of the swinging arm.
3. Loosen the chain adjuster, remove the support, push the wheel forward, and take off the chain from the sprocket.
4. Move the wheel backward and remove it.

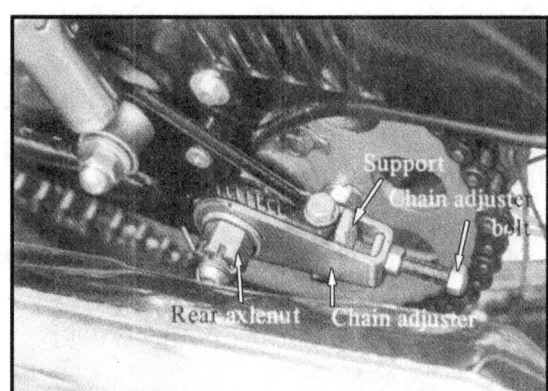

Fig. 9-4-1

9-5. Tire

The front tire is 3.00-19 and the rear tire is 3.50-18.
* Tire wear limits.
  Because tires affect the high-speed safety directly, please encourage users (your customers) to strictly observe the wear limits given below.

Tire wear limit .... Depth of tread { Front 1.6mm
Rear 2.0mm

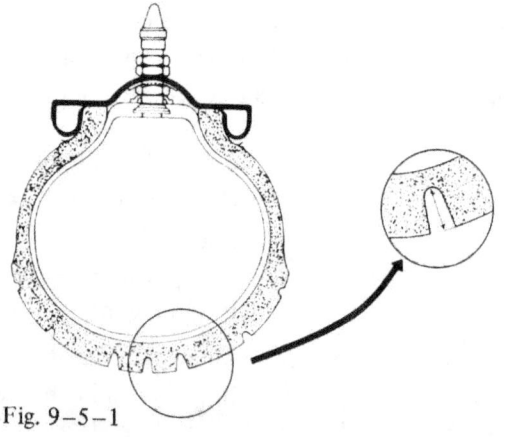

Fig. 9-5-1

10. TIGHTENING TORQUE

	Part	Tightening torque	
		kg-cm	lb-ft
1	Front axle nut	360-520	26-38
2	Front axle stopper nut	130-230	9.5-17
3	Rear axle nut	540-800	39-58
4	Steering stem head bolt (right & left)	180-300	13-23
5	Steering stem head bolt (rear side)	90-140	6.5-10
6	Steering stem bolt	200-300	14-23
7	Handle clamp bolt	90-200	6.5-14
8	Rear shock absorber (upper & lower)	180-280	13-20
9	Swinging arm pivot nut	500-750	36-54
10	Front & Rear brake cam lever nut	40-70	2.9-5.1
11	Rear torque link nut	180-280	13-20
12	Front footrest bolt	300-450	23-33
13	Front torque link	180-280	13-21
14	Engine mounting bolt, nut	300-400	23-29
15	Engine mounting plate bolt	130-230	9.5-17

Tightening torque for general bolts

Bolt diameter (mm)	Tightening torque			
	Usual bolt		"S" marked bolt	
	kg-cm	lb-ft	kg-cm	lb-ft
	20 – 40	1.5 – 2.9	30 – 60	2.2 – 4.4
6	40 – 70	2.9 – 5.1	60 – 100	4.4 – 7.3
8	90 – 140	6.6 – 10	130 – 230	9.5 – 17
10	180 – 280	13 – 20	250 – 400	18 – 29

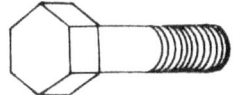

Usual bolt

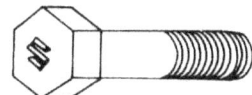

"S" marked bolt

11. IMPORTANT FUNCTIONAL PARTS

For safety driving of motorcycle, it is highly requested to check up the important items in accordance with following check list taking opportunity of periodical inspection.

Check list of important functional parts for safety driving.

	Item	Check for
Fuel system	Fuel hose Fuel tank	Fuel leakage
Suspension system	Front fork ass'y	Crack, Faulty welding of bracket
	Front fork comp. Front fork upper bracket	Crack, Faulty welding
	Front axle Rear axle	Crack
	Rear swinging arm	Crack, Faulty welding
Steering	Handlebar Handlebar upper clamp Handlebar lower clamp	Crack
Braking system	Front hub drum Rear hub drum Front hub panel Rear hub panel	Crack
	Rear torque link	Crack
	Front brake shoe Rear brake shoe	Crack, Peeling off of lining
	Front brake cam shaft Rear brake cam shaft	Crack, Deformation of serration
	Rear brake rod	Crack
	Brake pedal	Crack, Faulty welding
	Brake lever	Crack
	Front brake cable ass'y	Detachment of cable end
Frame	Frame	Crack, Faulty welding

PERIODICAL INSPECTION LIST

The chart below indicates time when inspections, adjustments and maintenance are required based on the distance the motorcycle runs, that is first 1,000 km (750 mi), and every 3,000 km (2,000 mi), 6,000 km (4,000 mi) and 12,000 km (8,000 mi) thereafter. According to the chart, advise users to make the motorcycle checked and serviced at your shop. See the appropriate section for instructions on making the inspection.

Service	Distance (km) / Distance (mi)	1,000 km / 750 mi	Every 3,000 km / Every 2,000 mi	Every 6,000 km / Every 4,000 mi	Every 12,000 km / Every 8,000 mi
Oil pump		Check operation, adjust control lever adjusting marks	Check operation, adjust control lever adjusting marks		
Spark plug		Clean	Clean and adjust gap	Replace	
Gearbox oil		Change	Change		
Throttle clutch and brake cables		Adjust play	Adjust play	Lubricate	
Carburetor		Adjust with throttle valve screw and pilot air screw	Adjust with throttle valve screw and pilot air screw		Overhaul and clean
Contact point breaker ass'y		Check contact point gap and ignition timing	Check contact point gap and ignition timing. Lubricate contact breaker cam oil felt.		Replace contact point
Cylinder head and cylinder		Retighten cylinder and cylinder head nuts	Retighten cylinder and cylinder head nuts	Remove carbon	
Battery		Check and service electrolyte solution	Check and service electrolyte solution		
Fuel cock		Clean fuel strainer		Clean fuel strainer	
Drive chain		Wash, then adjust and lubricate	Wash, then adjust and lubricate	Wash, then adjust and lubricate	
Brakes		Adjust play	Adjust play		
Air cleaner			Clean		
Throttle grip				Put grease in throttle grip	
Clutch		Adjust	Adjust		
Muffler		Retighten exhaust pipe clamp fitting nuts	Retighten exhaust pipe clamp fitting nuts	Remove carbon	
Steering stem		Check play / Retighten stem nut		Check play / Retighten stem nut	
Bolts, nuts and spokes		Retighten		Retighten	
Tire			Check the tire tread condition		

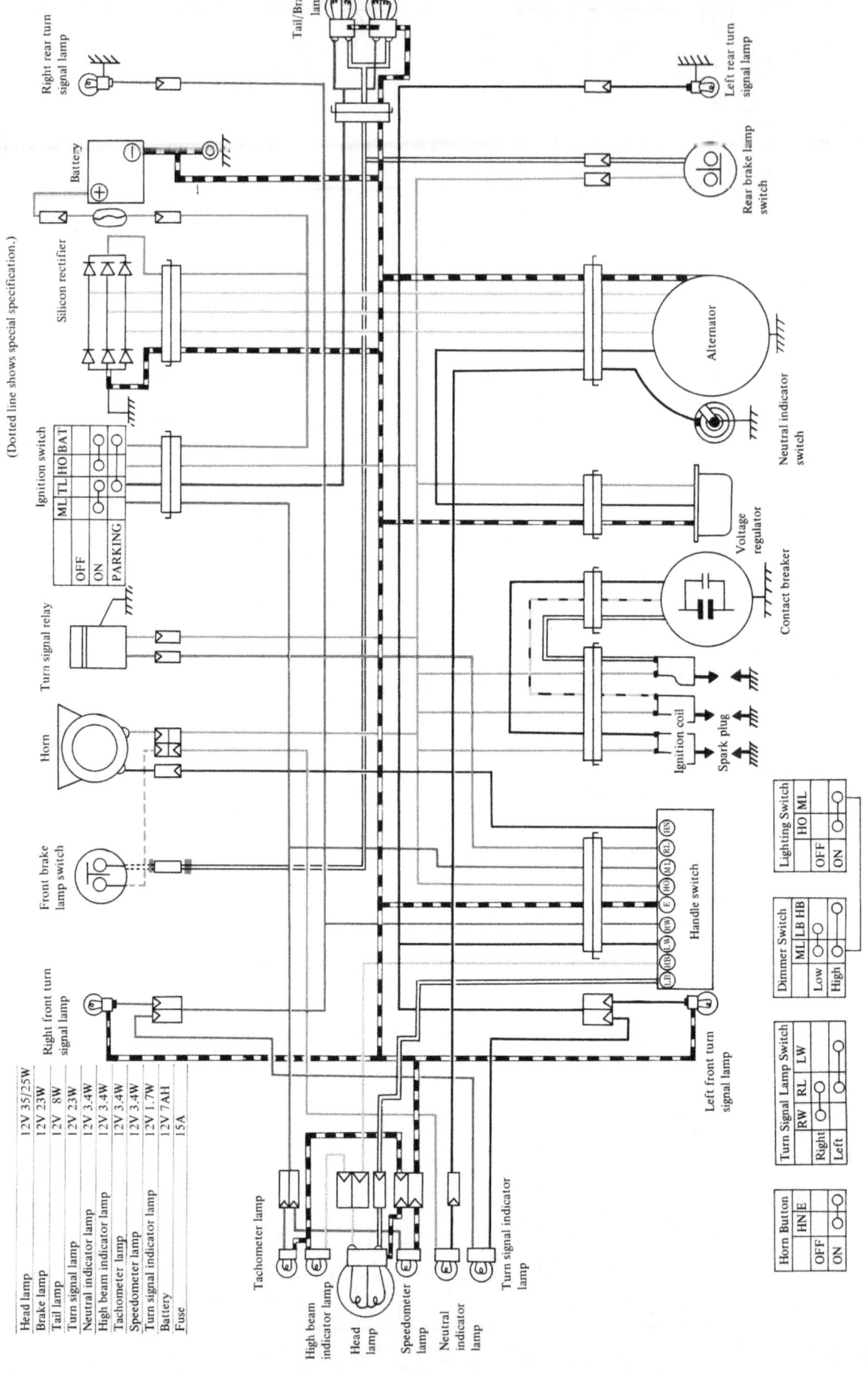

EXPLODED VIEW OF ENGINE (SUZUKI GT380)

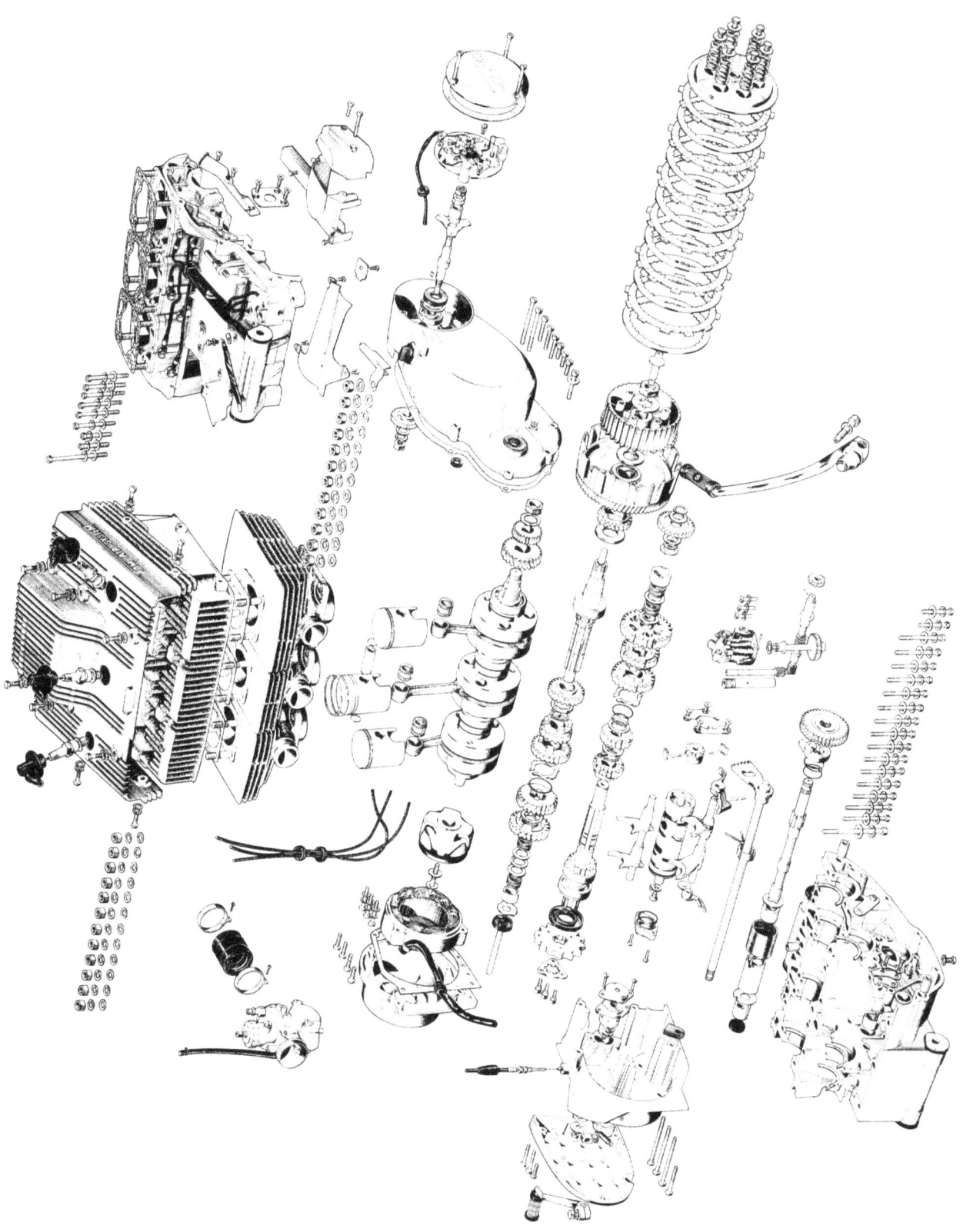

SUZUKI SERVICE MANUAL

MODEL

DISC BRAKE

FOREWORD

The purpose of this service manual is to provide a detailed description on the construction, operating principles, and adjusting and operating methods of the hydraulic disc brakes which have been recently adopted to Models GT125, GT185, GT250, GT380, GT550 and GT750.

To ensure a safe operation of these models capable of high-speed performance, an adequate maintenance of the brakes is vital. This manual is presented in the simplest possible manner so that the materials included are easily comprehensive to you. We hope that correct maintenance of these disc brakes will be facilitated most effectively by utilization of this manual.

Because this manual has been compiled on the models of the motorcycles available as of December, 1973, it is possible that the contents of this manual may not necessarily correspond to the motorcycles delivered to you due to possible changes of their specifications.

International Service Department
SUZUKI MOTOR CO.,LTD
December, 1973

FEATURES OF DISC BRAKE

Compared with the conventional drum-type brakes, the hydraulic disc brake has the following features:

- *Heat radiation from the friction surfaces is quite effective since the discs rotate in direct contact with the air. Therefore, stable brake power can always be provided, even if the disc brake is used repeatedly at high speeds.*

- *A brake lever stroke remains always constant since none of the disc brake parts is subjected to any deformation due to elevated temperatures.*

- *Replacement of pads is simple and no troublesome adjustment is required.*

- *Steady brake performance is ensured, since, even if the disc is wet during running in rainy weather or on muddy road, the restoring ability of brake power is excellent due to the extreme pressure characteristics for pushing pads.*

- *It has a smooth operation, since it has little portion to be mechanically abrased.*

INDEX

1. SPECIFICATION AND SERVICE DATA 4

2. TROUBLE SHOOTING 5

3. OUTLINE OF HYDRAULIC DISC BRAKE 6

    3-1 General 6
    3-2 Operation of Master Cylinder 7
    3-3 Operation of Caliper 8

4. INSPECTION AND REPAIR 9

    4-1 Brake Fluid and Its Handling 9
    4-2 Inspection and Replacing Method of Pads 10
    4-3 Master Cylinder, Brake Hose and Brake Pipe 13
    4-4 Caliper 19
    4-5 Brake Disc 22
    4-6 Periodic Replacement Parts 23

5. TIGHTENING TORQUE 24

6. SPECIAL TOOLS FOR DISC BRAKE 25

    6-1 Special Tools 25
    6-2 Necessary Materials 25

1. SPECIFICATION AND SERVICE DATA

Item	GT125 GT185 S.T.D. figure	GT125 GT185 Limit	GT250 GT380 S.T.D. figure	GT250 GT380 Limit	GT550 S.T.D. figure	GT550 Limit	GT750 S.T.D. figure	GT750 Limit
Disc thickness, front brake	5.00 mm (0.197 in.)	under 4.00 mm (0.157 in.)	7.00 mm (0.276 in.)	under 6.00 mm (0.236 in.)	7.00 mm (0.276 in.)	under 6.00 mm (0.236 in.)	7.00 mm (0.276 in.)	under 5.00 mm (0.236 in.)
Disc runout front brake	max. 0.1 mm (0.004 in.)	over 0.3 mm (0.012 in.)	max. 0.1 mm (0.004 in.)	over 0.3 mm (0.012 in.)	max. 0.1 mm (0.004 in.)	over 0.3 mm (0.012 in.)	max. 0.1 mm (0.004 in.)	over 0.3 mm (0.012 in.)
Outer diameter brake disc	250 mm (9.843 in.)		275 mm (10.827 in.)		295 mm (11.614 in.)		295 mm (11.614 in.)	
Inner diameter, master cylinder	14.00 to 14.04 mm (0.551 to 0.553 in.)	over 14.05 mm (0.553 in.)	14.00 to 14.04 mm (0.551 to 0.553 in.)	over 14.05 mm (0.553 in.)	14.00 to 14.04 mm (0.551 to 0.553 in.)	over 14.05 mm (0.553 in.)	15.87 to 15.91 mm (0.625 to 0.626 in.)	over 15.92 mm (0.627 in.)
Piston diameter, master cylinder	13.96 to 13.98 mm (0.550 to 0.551 in.)	under 13.94 mm (0.549 in.)	13.96 to 13.98 mm (0.550 to 0.551 in.)	under 13.94 mm (0.549 in.)	13.96 to 13.98 mm (0.550 to 0.551 in.)	under 13.94 mm (0.549 in.)	15.83 to 15.85 mm (0.623 to 0.624 in.)	under 15.81 mm (0.622 in.)
Inner diameter caliper cylinder	38.18 to 38.20 mm (1.503 to 1.504 in.)	over 38.22 mm (1.504 in.)	38.18 to 38.20 mm (1.503 to 1.504 in.)	over 38.22 mm (1.504 in.)	38.18 to 38.20 mm (1.503 to 1.504 in.)	over 38.22 mm (1.504 in.)	38.18 to 38.20 mm (1.503 to 1.504 in.)	over 38.22 mm (1.504 in.)
Piston diameter caliper cylinder	38.15 to 38.18 mm (1.502 to 1.503 in.)	under 38.10 mm (1.500 in.)	38.15 to 38.18 mm (1.502 to 1.503 in.)	under 38.10 mm (1.500 in.)	38.15 to 38.18 mm (1.502 to 1.503 in.)	under 38.10 mm (1.500 in.)	38.15 to 38.18 mm (1.502 to 1.503 in.)	under 38.10 mm (1.500 in.)
Effective diameter, front brake disc	199 mm (7.835 in.)		224 mm (8.819 in.)		244 mm (9.606 in.)		244 mm (9.606 in.)	
Effective brake lining area	19cm² x 2 pcs. (2.95 in² x 2 pcs.)		19cm² x 2 pcs. (2.95 in² x 2 pcs.)		19cm² x 2 pcs. (2.95 in² x 2 pcs.)		19cm² x 4 pcs. (2.95 in² x 4 pcs.)	
Type, front brake	Right-hand, hydraulic, single disc brake		Right-hand, hydraulic, single disc brake		Right-hand, hydraulic, single disc brake		Right-hand, hydraulic, double disc brake	
Type, caliper	Floating caliper, single cylinder		Floating caliper, single cylinder		Floating caliper, single cylinder		Floating caliper, single cylinder	

2. TROUBLE SHOOTING

Symptom and possible cause	Countermeasure
1. Insufficient brake power	
1) Leakage of brake fluid from hydraulic system	Repair or replace
2) Worn pads	Replace
3) Oil adhesion on engaged surface of pads	Clean disc and pads
4) Worn disc	Replace
5) Instruded air in hydraulic system	Bleed air
2. Brake squeaking	
1) Carbon adhesion on pad surface	Repair surface with sandpaper
2) Tilted pad	Modify pad fitting
3) Damaged wheel bearing	Replace
4) Loosened front-wheel axle	Tighten with regular torque
5) Worn pads	Replace
6) Intruded foreign substance into brake fluid	Replace brake fluid
7) Clogged return port of master cylinder	Disassemble and clean master cylinder
3. Excessive brake lever stroke	
1) Intruded air into hydraulic system	Bleed air
2) Worn brake lever cam	Replace brake lever
3) Insufficient brake fluid	Replenish fluid to normal level; bleed air
4) Improper quality of brake fluid	Replace by proper one
4. Leakage of brake fluid	
1) Insufficient tightening of connection joints	Tighten with regular torque
2) Cracked pipe	Replace
3) Worn piston and/or cup	Replace piston and/or cup

3. OUTLINE OF HYDRAULIC DISC BRAKE

3-1 General

The hydraulic disc brake adopted in Suzuki's models GT125, GT185, GT250, GT380, GT550 and GT750 consists of four main portions, i.e., brake discs mounted on a front wheel hub, a master cylinder for pressurizing, a brake hose line for fluid pressure, and a caliper which presses pads to brake disc by means of hydraulic pressures.

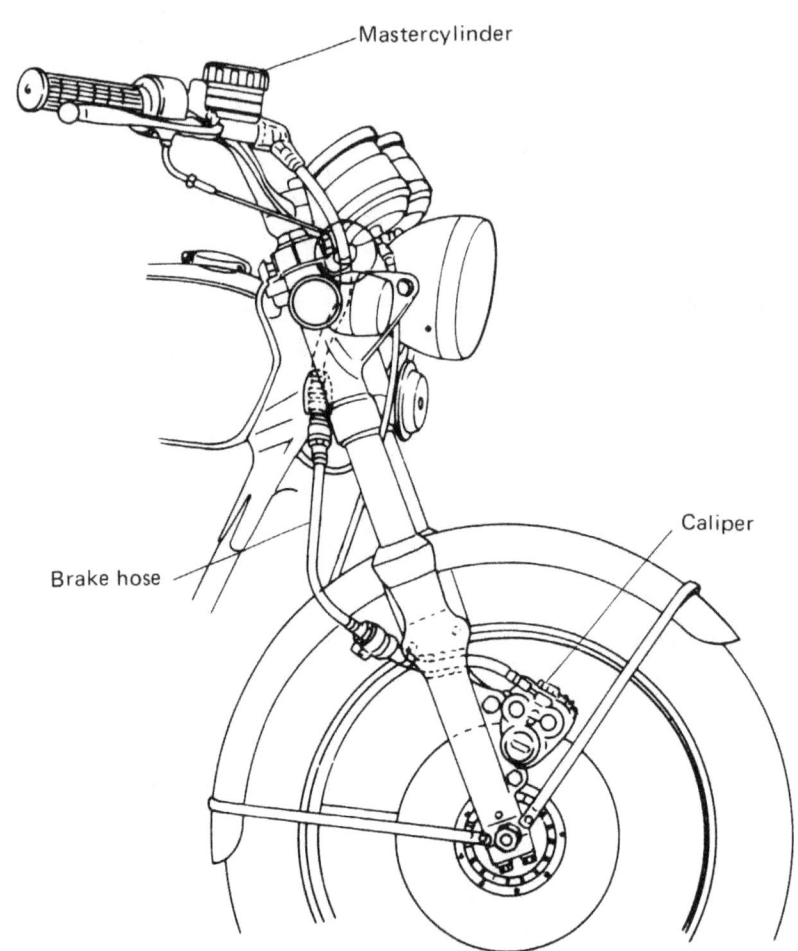

Fig. 3-1-1

3-2 Operation of Master Cylinder

3-2-1 Squeezing brake lever

The piston ③ is pushed in the direction of arrow by the brake cam ② when the brake lever is squeezed. The primary cup ④ also moves together with the piston and when it closes the return port ⑤ which is provided at the master cylinder body, brake fluid in front of the primary cup begins to be pressurized and delivered to the caliper by opening the check valve ⑥ with its pressure.

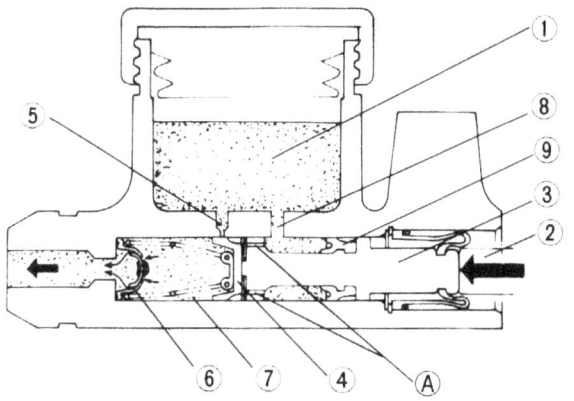

1 Reservoir	6 Check valve
2 Brake lever cam	7 Spring
3 Piston	8 Inlet port
4 Primary cup	9 Secondary cup
5 Return port	

Fig. 3-2-1

3-2-2 Releasing brake lever

As soon as the brake lever is released, the piston is pushed back by the spring ⑦. Because the brake fluid from the caliper may not return to the master cylinder immediately due to its flow resistance, hydraulic pressure inside the cylinder is reduced momentarily and fluid flows from the reservoir to the front section of the primary cup through the inlet port ⑧, three small holes Ⓐ on the piston flange and the circumference of the primary cup.

Then high pressure brake fluid from the caliper releases the check valve body from its contact with the outlet part allowing to have the clearance for a fluid passage. A small amount of the fluid returns from the caliper to the master cylinder through the clearance thus made by the movement of the check valve body.

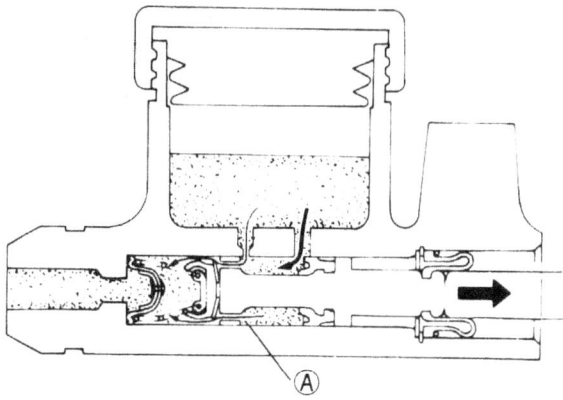

Fig. 3-2-2

3-2-3 After completing return stroke of brake lever

A large amount of the brake fluid having been delivered to the caliper returns to the reservoir through the clearance behind the check valve base and the return port on the master cylinder body.

As the brake fluid from the caliper returns to the reservoir, hydraulic pressure in the brake hose is reduced gradually and the spring tension surmounts the hydraulic pressure of the brake hose resulting in closing the clearance behind the check valve base. However, some fluid pressure still remains in the brake hose because of the initial tension of the spring. Brake fluid continues to flow into the reservoir through a small notch provided around the periphery of the check valve body and the return port. The master cylinder completes its operation when residual pressure in the brake hose vanishes completely.

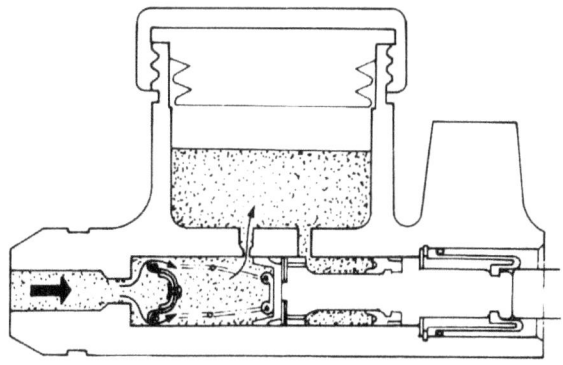

Fig. 3-2-3

3-3 Operation of Caliper

3-3-1 Squeezing brake lever

Brake fluid from the master cylinder delivered under pressure flows into the caliper cylinder through inlet portion Ⓐ of the caliper and pushes piston ① in the direction of arrow.

The pushed piston moves together with the pad No.1 (moving side) ② in this direction until it can not move any further forward due to the pad No.1 hitting brake disc ③.

As soon as the pad No.1 touches the brake disc so that the piston may not move any further, the caliper body floating on the caliper axle is pushed in reverse direction by the fluid pressure in the cylinder and moves in the right side direction as shown in Fig. 3-3-2.

Since the pad No.2 (stationary side) ④ is mounted to the caliper body, the disc is subjected to a powerful braking force with pads Nos.1 and 2 depressing the disc from opposite directions respectively.

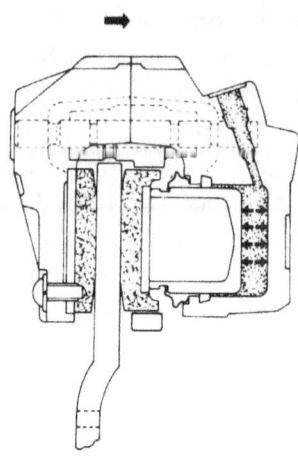

Fig. 3-3-2

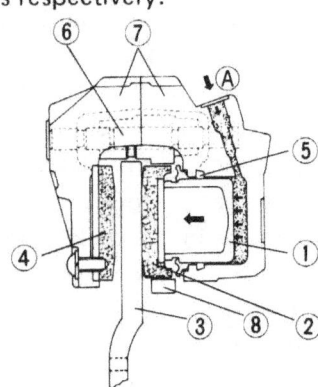

1 Piston	5 Piston seal
2 Pad No. 1	6 Caliper axle
3 Brake disc	7 Caliper body
4 Pad No. 2	8 Caliper holder

Fig. 3-3-1

3-3-2 Releasing brake lever

When the brake lever is released and fluid pressure in the caliper cylinder vanishes, the piston moves in the direction of arrow in Fig. 3-3-3, being pushed by piston seal ⑤ which was pressed onto the piston by fluid pressure and is now restoring its original shape with fluid pressure released. Therefore, the pads pressed to the disc part from the disc since the piston moves as much as the piston seal displacement, thus setting the brake disc free.

3-3-3 Self adjusting of clearance between pads and disc

If the traveling distance of piston exceeds the displacement of the piston seal, the piston is moved as far as the braking stroke while the piston slides between itself and the piston seal, whereas a return stroke of the piston due to the piston seal restoration after brake release is always constant and the returned position of the piston relatively varies with the wear of pads.

Consequently, clearance between the pads and the piston, or between the pads and the brake disc is always kept constant regardless of the condition of pad wear.

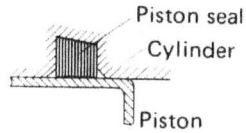

When brake lever is released

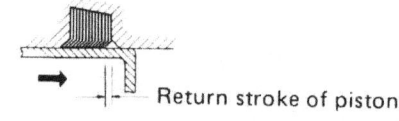

When brake lever is squeezed

Fig. 3-3-3

4. INSPECTION AND REPAIR

4-1 Brake Fluid and Its Handling

4-1-1 Inspecting brake fluid level

Be sure to check brake fluid level in the reservoir. In inspecting brake fluid, first mount your motorcycle firmly onto the center stand with its handlebar kept straight up without fail. If the level is found to be lower than the level mark ① provided on the reservoir, replenish the reservoir with one of the brake fluid graded below.

Specification & Classification	Remarks
DOT 3	in U.S.A.
DOT 4	in U.S.A.
SAE J1703a	
SAE J1703b	
SAE J170c	
SAE 70R3	A classification in obsolete specification of SAE J70b.

Note: Since the brake system of these motorcycles is filled with a glycol base brake fluid by the manufacturer, do not use or mix different types of fluid such as silicone-based and petroleum-based fluid for refilling the system, otherwise damage sustained will be serious.
Do not use any brake fluid taken from old or used, or unsealed containers.
Do not squeeze the brake lever while the reservoir cap is removed, otherwise brake fluid will sometimes spout out. Do not put the removed reservoir cap on the speedometer or tachometer. Brake fluid will damage the paint surface and instrument gauge lenses.
Take due care especially so that water may not enter brake fluid on rainy day particularly during replacement or in handling a brake fluid container, because brake fluid has hygroscopic property, and its boiling point falls excessively if water is mixed with it.

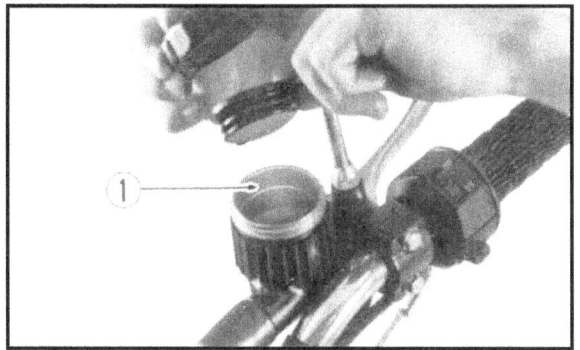

(All "K" models)   Fig. 4-1-1

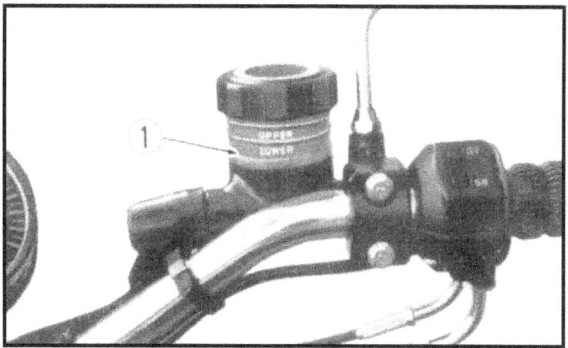

(All "L" models)   Fig. 4-1-2

4-1-2 Air bleeding from brake system

If the brake lever travel becomes excessive or the lever feels a soft or spongy feeling, you must carry out air bleeding from the brake system in the following procedure:
It is best if two persons perform this.

1) Attach the bleeder tube to the bleeder valve after removing the bleeder valve dust cap as shown in Fig. 4-1-3. A transparent tube is useful in finding air bubble expelled from the system.
2) The tube must be submerged in a clean container partially filled with brake fluid.
3) Fill the reservoir with the aforementioned brake fluid.

Note: Keep at least one half full of fluid in the reservoir during the bleeding procedure.

Fig. 4-1-3

4) Screw in the cap on the reservoir to prevent a spout of brake fluid and entry of dust.
5) Allow the pressure in the hydraulic system by squeezing rapidly the brake lever several times and then holding the lever tight.
6) Unscrew (open) the bleeder valve by one half turn and squeeze the lever all the way down. Do not release the lever until the bleeder valve is screwed in (closed) again.
7) Repeat steps 5) and 6) until air bubbles disappear in the bleeder tube or container and screw in (close) the bleeder valve securely.
8) Remove the tube and install the bleeder valve dust cap.
9) Check the fluid level in the reservoir and replenish if necessary, after the bleeding operation has been completed.
10) Reinstall the diaphragm and the diaphragm plate and tighten the reservoir cap securely.

Caution: Do not reuse the brake fluid drained from the system.

For model GT750, bleed air at first from the left-hand side caliper and then from the right according to the aforementioned procedure.

4-1-3 Changing brake fluid

Boiling point of brake fluid falls considerably with absorption of moisture which may take place during a long period of use. Therefore, it is recommended to exchange old brake fluid with new one periodically.

Exchange interval: One year

On changing brake fluid, extreme attention should be paid so as not to mix any foreign materials because they would block the return port of the master cylinder resulting in the brake dragging or squeaking.
When brake fluid is to be changed, perform the following procedure.
1) Attach a bleeder tube to the bleeder valve. Drain out old brake fluid by squeezing the brake lever with the bleeder valve opened until the brake fluid disappears in the bleeder tube.

2) After old brake fluid is drained out from the system completely, carry out the same procedure as described in "4-1-2 Air bleeding".

4-2 Inspection and Replacing Method of Pads

4-2-1 Inspection of pads

Check worn condition of the friction pads. If any of the friction pads is worn out up to the red limit line ① marked on its circumference, replace it following the procedure of "4-2-2" or "4-2-3".

Caution: Wash mud and dust off around the front wheel and/or caliper prior to the replacing operation.

Fig. 4-2-1

4-2-2 Replacing of pads for models GT125, GT185, GT250, GT380 or GT550

1) Set up the center stand and load at the rear portion to let the front wheel free.
2) Remove the front wheel assembly.
3) Unscrew the pad fastening screw, and take off pad No. 2 (stationary side).

Fig. 4-2-2

4) Squeeze the brake lever two or three times gradually to force out pad No. 1 by fluid pressure while observing the motion of pad.

Fig. 4-2-3

5) Apply "Brake Pad Grease", which is provided as a component of Pad Set as shown in Fig. 4-2-4, onto the periphery and back plate of pad No. 1 as illustrated in Fig. 4-2-5 in a very thin layer.

Caution: Do not use another grease.
Apply grease thinly so as not to flow out, otherwise resulting in reduced brake performance.

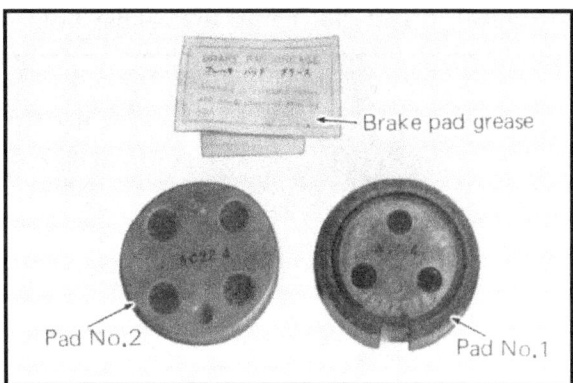

Fig. 4-2-4

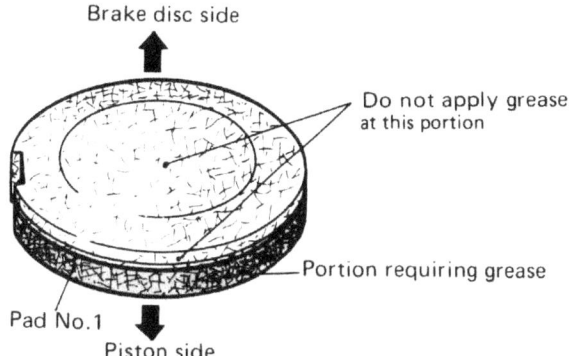

Fig. 4-2-5

Note: The pad set supplied as a repair part is classified into three types according to the shape of Pad No. 1. The following table shows part numbers and the shapes of Pad No. 1. When replacing this part, refer to this table and be careful not to assemble erroneously.

Shape of pad	Parts No.	Model to which pad is applicable
Flat	59100–36830	GT125L, GT185L
Indentification mark "A" / Depth 1.5mm (0.06 in.)	59100–18840	Models GT250L, GT380L, GT550L and GT550K with engine serial numbers 32292 and thereafter, and models GT750L and GT750K with engine serial numbers 38591 and thereafter.
Depth 2.8 mm (0.11 in.)	59100–31830	Models GT250K, GT380K and GT550K with engine serial numbers 32291 and before, and model GT750K with engine serial numbers 38590 and before.

6) Push in pad No. 1 into the caliper holder.

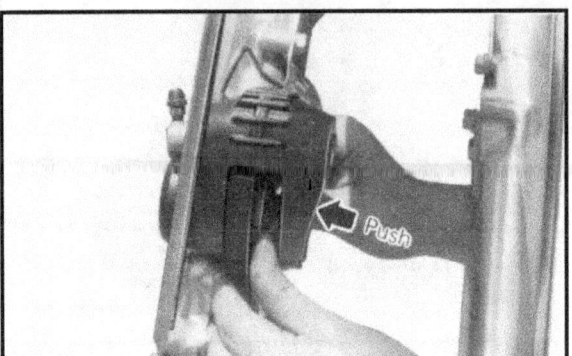

Fig. 4-2-6

7) Mount pad No. 2 to the caliper body.

Caution: Do not apply any grease to the pad No. 2, and take care not to mount it inclined.

8) Install the front wheel assembly to the front fork.
9) Squeeze the brake lever two or three times to confirm its operation, and bleed air if necessary.

4-2-3 Replacing of pad for model GT750

1) Take off the left brake pipe cover ① and pipe guide ②.

Fig. 4-2-7

2) Loosen the two left caliper fitting bolts ③.

Fig. 4-2-8

3) Detach the left caliper with the brake pipe connected and fix it on the front fork by string or hold it unmoved so as not to bend the brake pipe.

Fig. 4-2-9

4) Take off the front wheel assembly.
5) Mount the removed left caliper to the front fork
6) Insert a spacer ④ between pads Nos. 1 and 2 of the right caliper to stop piston movement and clip it with an elastic rubber ring ⑤ to prevent it from falling.

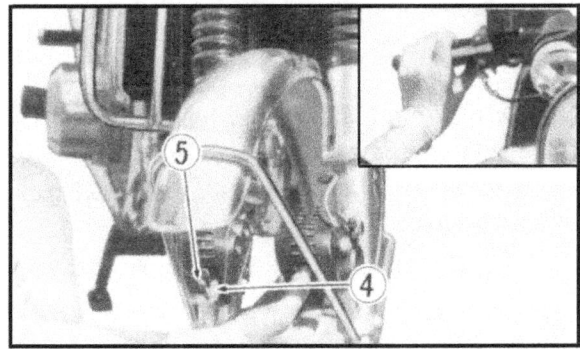

Fig. 4-2-10

7) Replace pads Nos. 1 and 2 of the left caliper in the same manner as for models GT125, GT185, GT250, GT380 and GT550.
8) Remove the spacer from the right caliper, and insert it in the left caliper.
9) Replace pads Nos. 1 and 2 of the right caliper.
10) Take off the left caliper and hold it.
11) Install the front wheel assembly to the front fork.
12) Mount the left caliper to the front fork.
13) Mount the left brake pipe cover and guide.
14) Squeeze the brake lever two or three times to confirm its operation, and bleed air if necessary.

Note: When replacing the front tire or repairing puncture, it is necessary to remove the left caliper before removing the front wheel assembly.

4-3 Master Cylinder, Brake Hose and Brake Pipe

4-3-1 General

Always check the master cylinder, brake hose and the brake pipe for operation and leakage of brake fluid since they are very important parts for safe riding.
If any abnormal condition is found, repair or replace. Though every part is made of material rigidly selected under high degree quality control, periodically replace the master cylinder piston cup and its related parts in order to always keep the motorcycle in its best condition.

Index No.	Description
1	Master cylinder assembly
2	Check valve
3	Spring
4	Primary cup
5	Secondary cup
6	Piston
7	Stop plate
8	Circlip
9	Boot
10	Boot plate
11	Boot stopper
12	Diaphragm
13	Diaphragm plate
14	Reservoir cap
15	Washer
16	Bolt
17	Master cylinder boot
18	Union bolt
19	Washer
20	Front brake hose
21	Brake hose guide
22	Grommet
23	Brake pipe
24	Brake hose guide
25	Grommet
26	Brake hose
27	Grommet

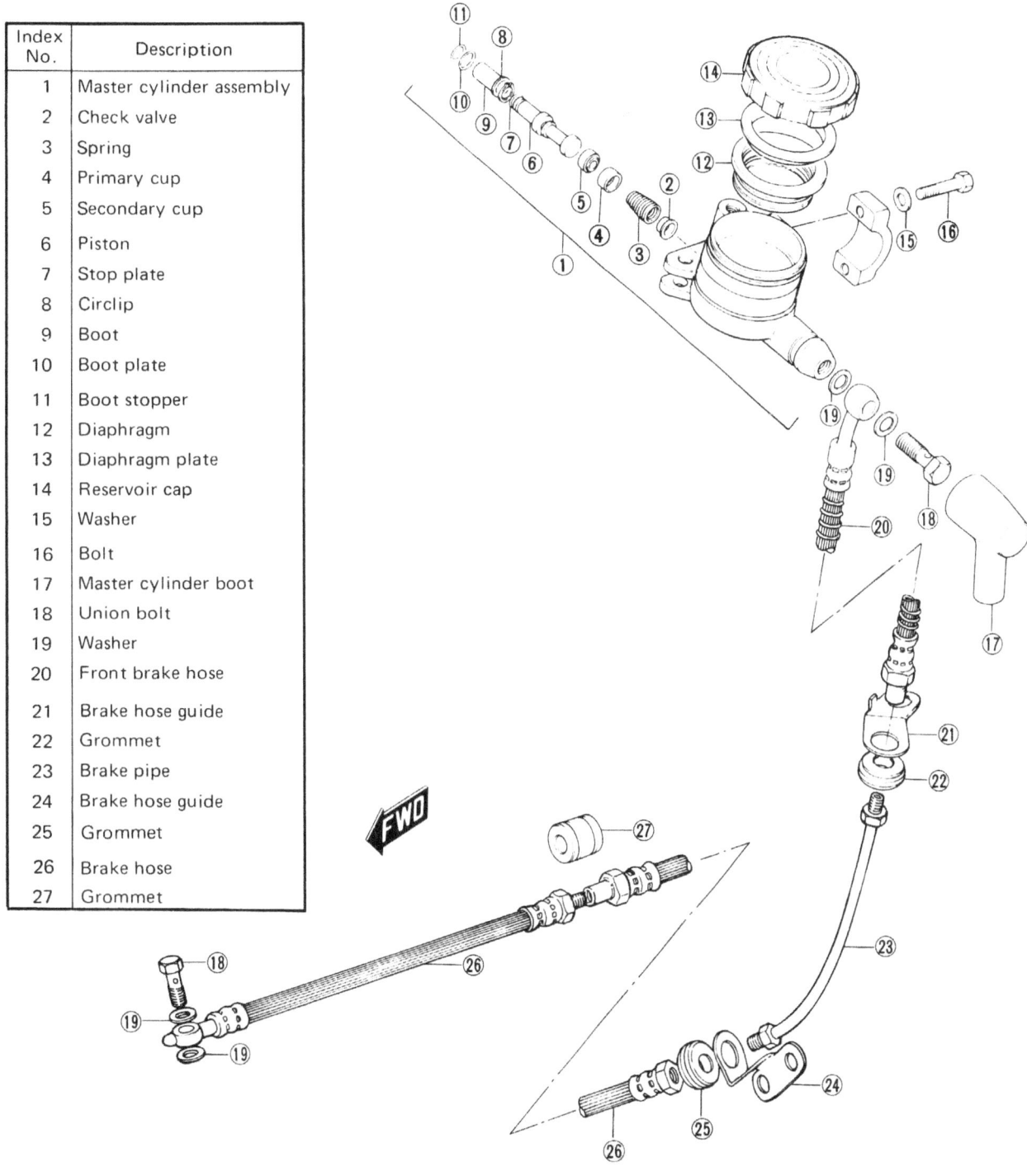

(GT125, GT185)　　　　　　　　Fig. 4-3-1

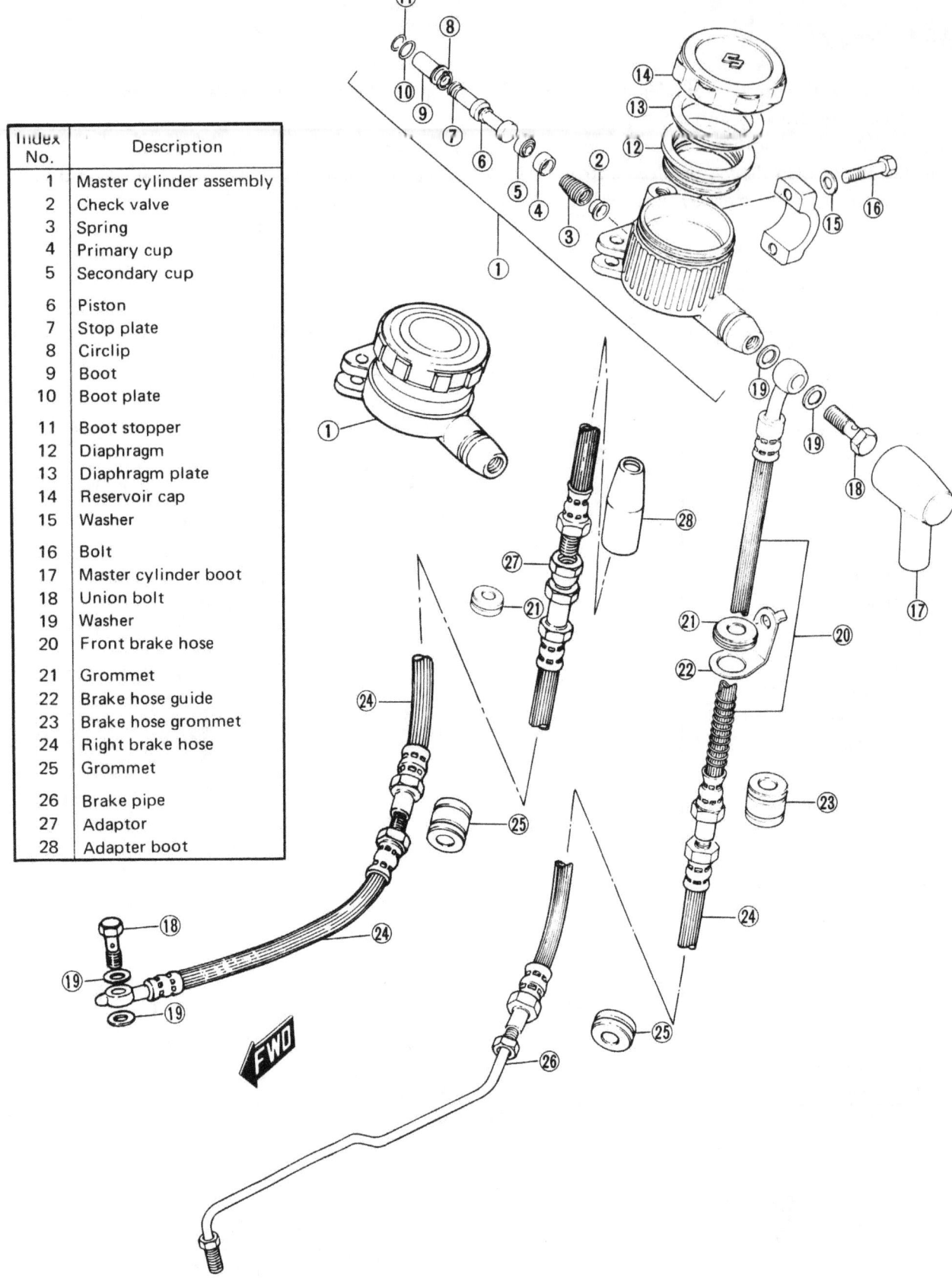

Index No.	Description
1	Master cylinder assembly
2	Check valve
3	Spring
4	Primary cup
5	Secondary cup
6	Piston
7	Stop plate
8	Circlip
9	Boot
10	Boot plate
11	Boot stopper
12	Diaphragm
13	Diaphragm plate
14	Reservoir cap
15	Washer
16	Bolt
17	Master cylinder boot
18	Union bolt
19	Washer
20	Front brake hose
21	Grommet
22	Brake hose guide
23	Brake hose grommet
24	Right brake hose
25	Grommet
26	Brake pipe
27	Adaptor
28	Adapter boot

(GT250, GT380 & GT550) Fig. 4-3-2

Index No.	Description
1	Master cylinder assembly
2	Check valve
3	Spring
4	Primary cup
5	Secondary cup
6	Piston
7	Plate stop
8	Circlip
9	Boot
10	Boot plate
11	Boot stopper
12	Diaphragm
13	Diaphragm plate
14	Reservoir cap
15	Bolt
16	Washer
17	Master cylinder boot
18	Union bolt
19	Washer
20	Grommet
21	Brake hose guide
22	Front brake hose
23	RH & LH brake hose
24	Three way joint
25	Grommet
26	RH brake pipe
27	LH brake pipe
28	Adapter
29	Adapter boot

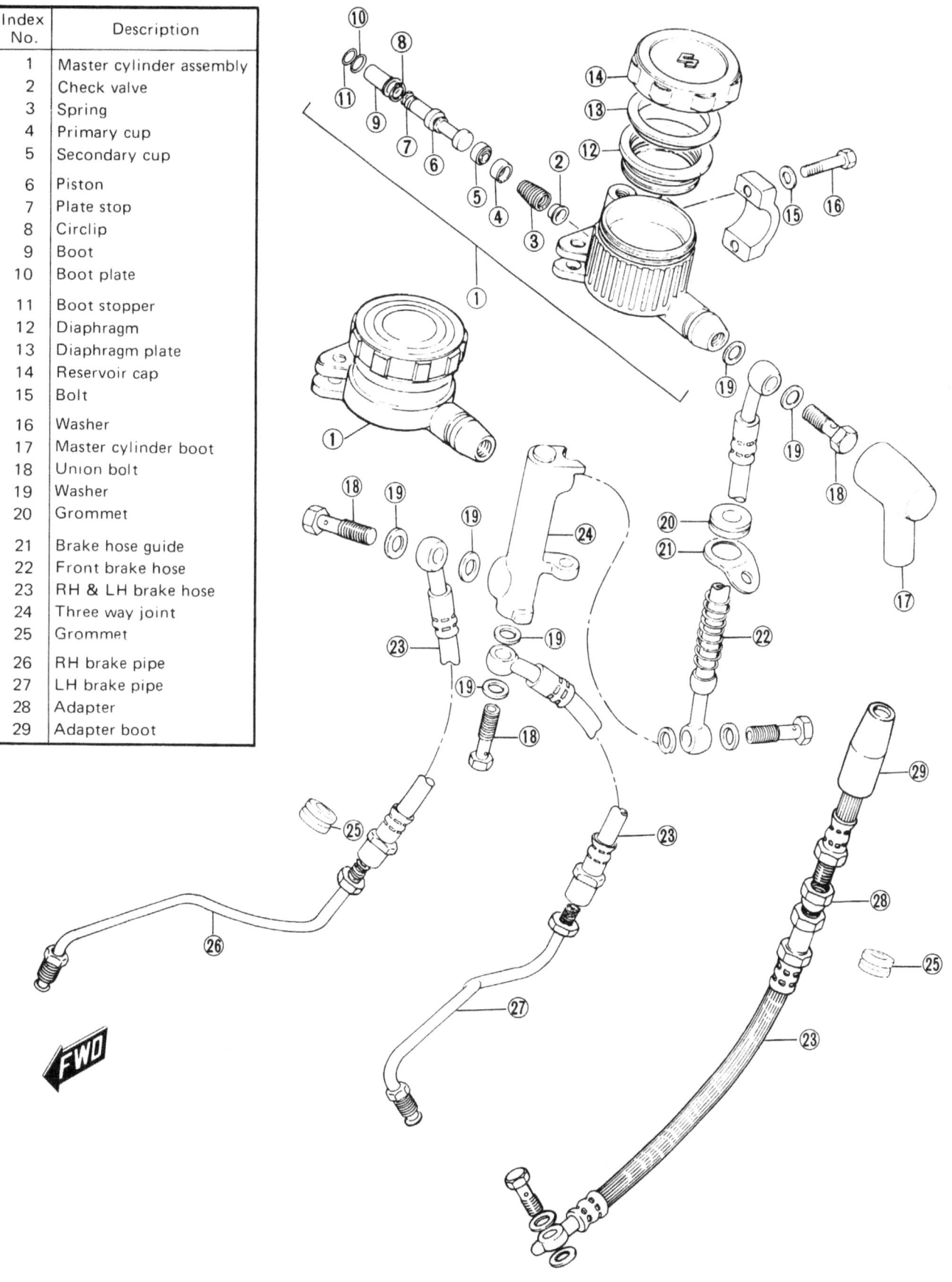

(GT750)   Fig. 4-3-3

4-3-2 Removing master cylinder

1) Remove the stop switch from the master cylinder (only for U.S.A. and Canadian specifications).

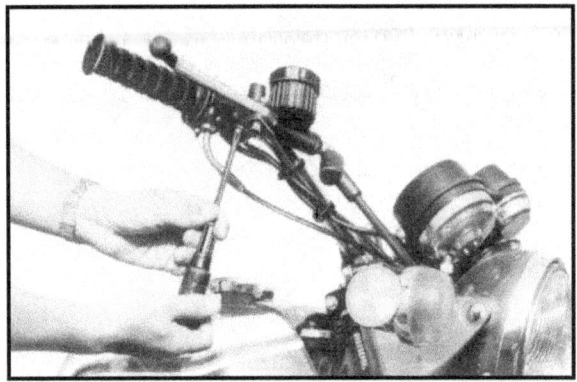

Fig. 4-3-3

2) Put a piece of rag beneath the union bolt on the master cylinder to catch drops of brake fluid. Unscrew the union bolt and disconnect the connection between the brake hose and the master cylinder.

Fig. 4-3-4

3) Unscrew two master cylinder fastening bolts and remove the master cylinder body from the handlebar.
4) Empty brake fluid out of the reservoir.

4-3-3 Disassembling master cylinder

1) Remove the brake lever.
2) Remove the boot stopper while taking care not to damage the boot and then remove the boot.

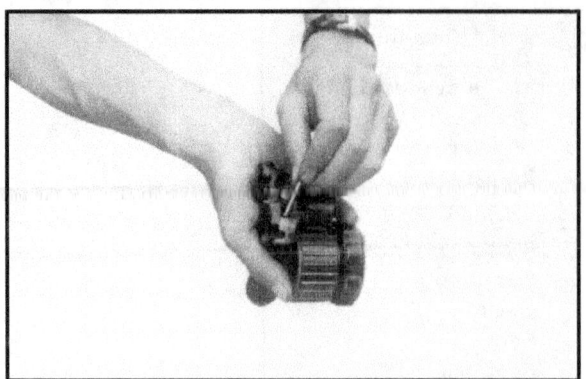

Fig. 4-3-5

3) Remove the circlip with the special tool (Circlip remover ① 19920 - 73110).

Fig. 4-3-6

4) Remove the piston, primary cup, spring and check valve.
5) Put the removed parts into a clean container and wash them in new brake fluid.

Caution: Never wash them in gasoline or petroleum; otherwise such fluid will damage rubber parts.

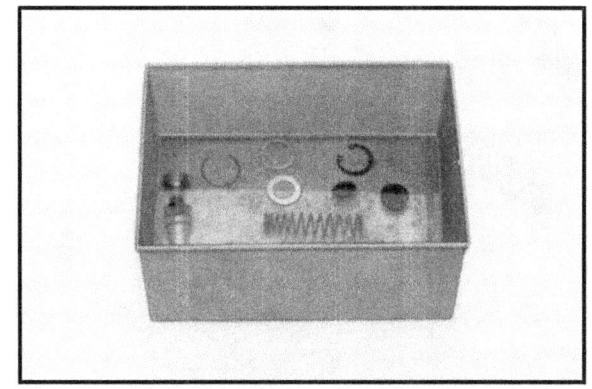

Fig. 4-3-7

4-3-4 Checking master cylinder

Replace the following parts with new one if any abnormality is found.

1) Master cylinder: Measure inner diameter of the master cylinder with an inside dial indicator.

Standard	Limit	Model
14.00 to 14.04 mm (0.551 to 0.553 in.)	Over 14.05 mm (0.553 in.)	GT125 GT185 GT250 GT380 GT550
15.87 to 15.91 mm (0.625 to 0.626 in.)	Over 15.92 mm (0.627 in.)	GT750

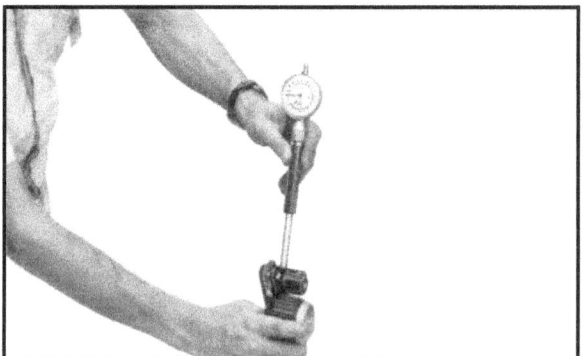

Fig. 4-3-8

2) Piston: Measure outer diameter of the piston.

Standard	Limit	Model
13.96 to 13.98 mm (0.550 to 0.551 in.)	Under 13.94 mm (0.549 in.)	GT125 GT185 GT250 GT380 GT550
15.83 to 15.85 mm (0.623 to 0.624 in.)	Under 15.81 mm (0.622 in.)	GT750

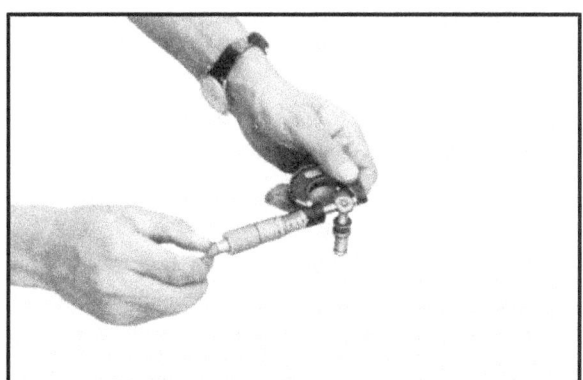

Fig. 4-3-9

3) Check valve: Inspect the check valve for operation.
4) O-ring (For models GT125L, GT185L, GT250L, GT380L, GT550L and GT750L):

Check the mating surfaces of the plastic reservoir and master cylinder proper for oil leaking.

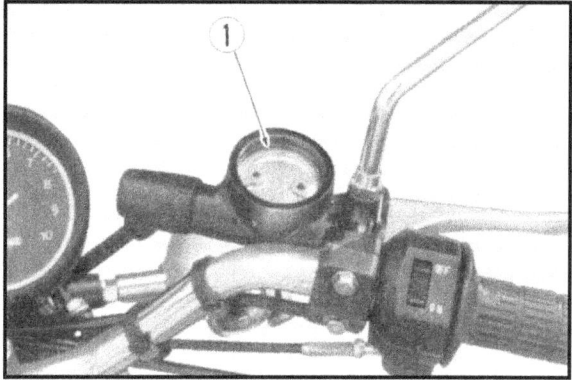

Fig. 4-3-10

4-3-5 Assembling master cylinder

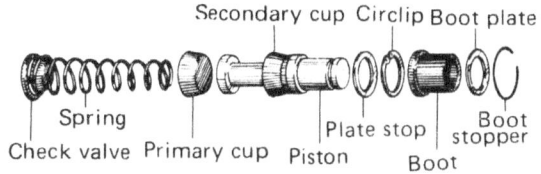

Fig. 4-3-11

Follow the removal procedures in the reverse order. When assembling them, pay attention to the following points.

1) Do not confuse the directions of assembling the primary cup. Refer to Fig. 4-3-11.
2) Replace a cotter pin of the brake lever pivot nut with new one and fit it securely.
3) Mount the master cylinder to the handlebar so that a gap between it and the switch box is about 2 mm (0.08 in.) and the reservoir becomes horizontal when the motorcycle is held on the center stand and steering is kept in a straight-on direction. Refer to Fig. 4-3-12.

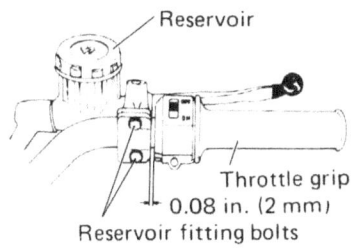

Fig. 4-3-12

4-3-6 Master cylinder identification mark

Cylinder bore of the master cylinder for model GT750 is larger than that for model GT125, GT185, GT250, GT380 or GT550. In order to easily distinguish the master cylinder for model GT750 from those for other models, an identification mark "D" is punched on the back of the reservoir.

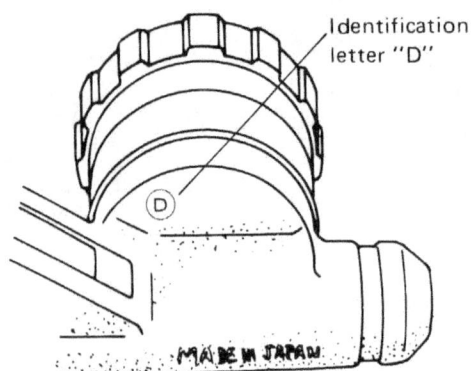

Fig. 4-3-13

4-3-7 Checking brake hose and pipe

Always check for the following items and replace immediately if any abnormality is found.
1) Damage to or swell of brake hose and/or pipe.
2) Traces of wear on the brake hose and/or pipe in contact with other parts.
3) Rusty brake pipe.
4) Fluid leakage at any joint of brake pipes and/or hose.

Note: If leakage should be found at any joint, retighten the bolts and nuts to the specified tightening torque. (Refer to page 24.)

4-3-8 Assembling brake hose and pipe

When connecting the brake hose and pipe, pay attention to the following points.
1) Be sure to use new brake pipe at all times when the brake pipe is assembled, because the cut end of the used brake pipe has been flared along the shape of the caliper inlet or the brake hose outlet as shown in Fig. 4-3-14. If the used pipe is reinstalled as it is, the air-tightness of the connection decreases, causing the brake fluid leakage.

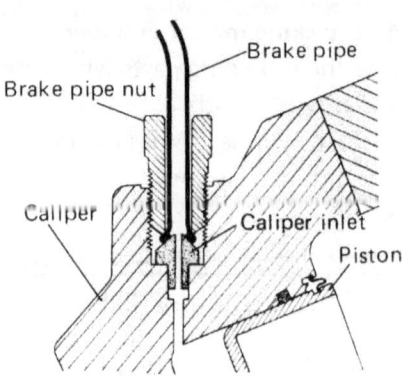

Fig. 4-3-14

2) When tightening two brake hose adapters, make sure that the hoses are free and not twisted. For models GT125L, GT185L, GT250K, GT380K, GT550K and GT750K which use brake pipe rather than hose, tighten the brake pipe adapter last of all. For models GT250L, GT380L, GT550L, and GT750L, first of all, remove twist from the hose, and then, tighten the hose joint with the brake hose adapter shown in Fig. 4-3-15.

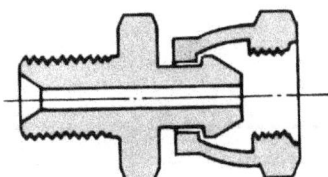

Fig. 4-3-15

3) When connecting the brake pipe to the caliper body, screw the nut in with your fingers to prevent stripping the threads, and then tighten it with a wrench to the specified torque.
4) Check that there is a generous space between each of them and the fuel tank, the front fork or other parts, and correct if any abnormality is found. Check that the hose or pipe does not contact any other parts particularly when the handlebar is turned fully to the right or left or when the front fork is brought down to the bottom.
5) After the assembling, check for no brake fluid leakage at any connection while holding the brake lever tightly.

4-4 Caliper

4-4-1 General

Index No.	Description
1	Caliper assembly
2	Caliper holder
3	Caliper stopper
4	Stopper rubber
5	Piston
6	Piston seal
7	Pad No.1 (moving side)
8	Pad No.2 (stationary side)
9	Screw
10	Lock washer
11	Caliper axle
12	Axle dust cover
13	Caliper axle "O" ring
14	Piston boot
15	Bleeder cap
16	Bleeder
17	Bolt
18	Washer
19	Lock washer
20	Caliper emblem

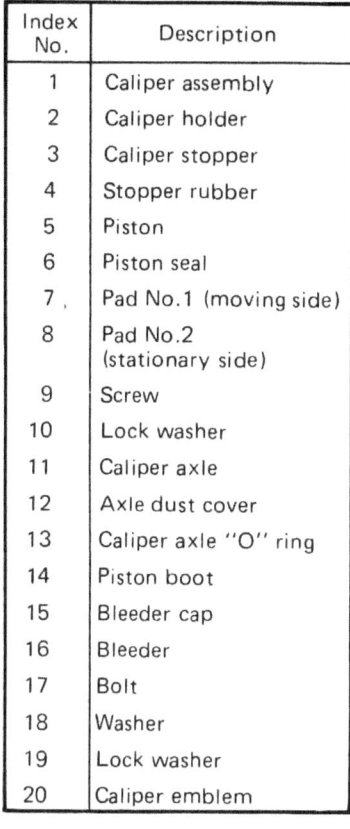

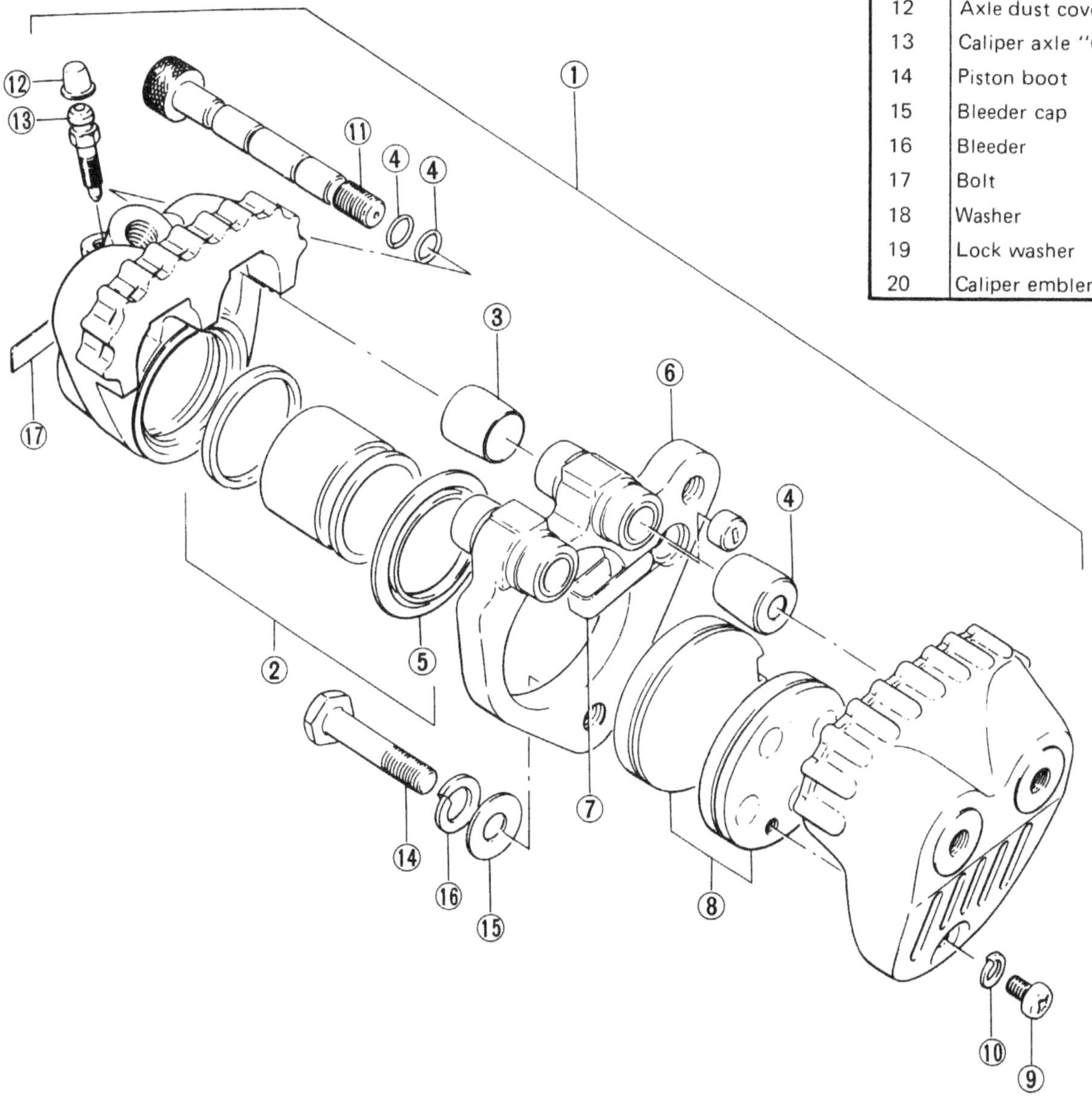

Fig. 4-4-1

4-4-2 Removing
1) Unscrew the brake pipe nut and caliper fastening bolts.
2) Pull out the caliper body from the disc plate.

4-4-3 Disassembling
1) Unscrew the caliper axle bolts with a special tool (8 mm hexagon L-type wrench 09900-06904) and separate the inner caliper body from the outer body.

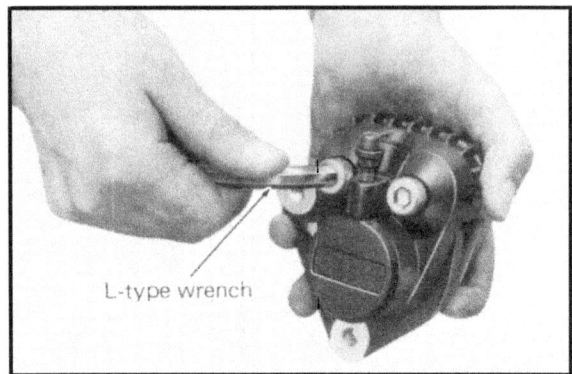

Fig. 4-4-2

2) Remove the caliper holder.
3) Remove "O" rings on the caliper axle.
4) Remove the caliper axles.
5) Remove the piston boot.
6) Push out the piston with compressed air while holding it with finger to prevent it from blowing out.

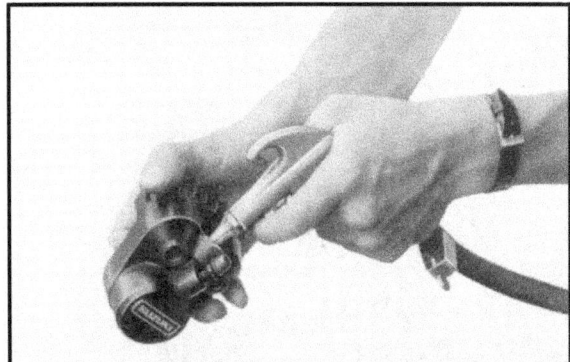

Fig. 4-4-3

7) Remove the piston seal as shown in Fig. 4-4-4.
8) Wash the piston, piston boot, piston seal and "O" rings of the caliper axles with new brake fluid. See Fig. 4-4-5.
   Caution: Never use gasoline or petroleum; otherwise rubber parts will be damaged.
   Do not wash the pads and also take care that brake fluid is not splashed onto the pads.

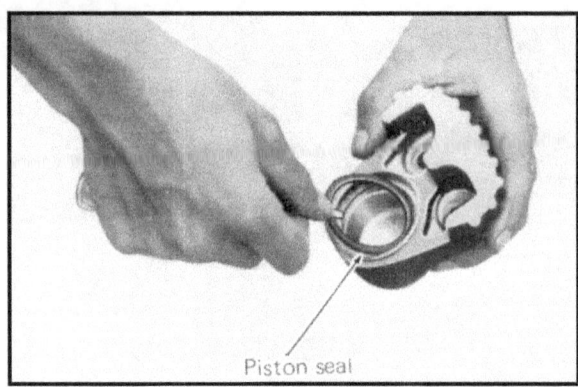

Fig. 4-4-4

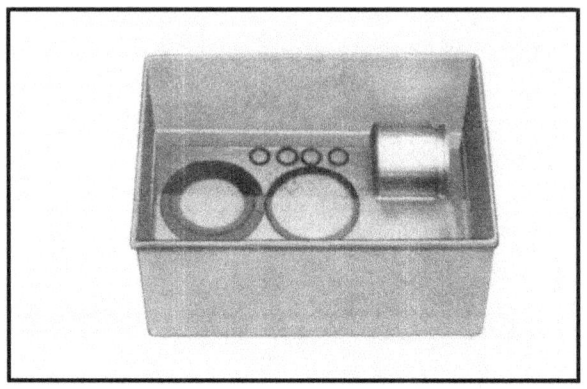

Fig. 4-4-5

4-4-4 Checking
When disassembling the caliper, check the following points and replace if any abnormality is found.
1) Cylinder: Its inner diameter is not worn out of its limit.

Standard	Limit	Model
38.18 to 38.20 mm (1.503 to 1.504 in.)	Over 38.22 mm (1.504 in.)	GT125 GT185 GT250 GT380 GT550 GT750

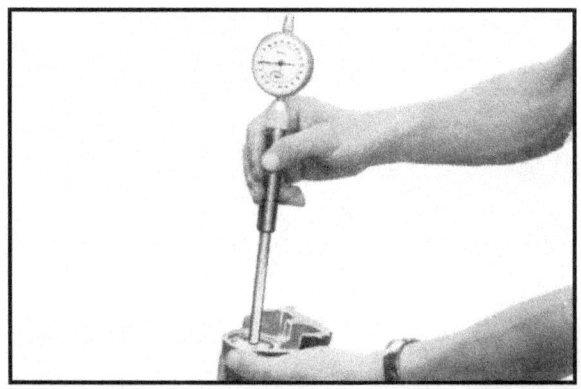

Fig. 4-4-6

2) Piston: Its outer diameter is not worn out of its limit.

Standard	Limit	Model
38.15 to 38.18 mm (1.502 to 1.503 in.)	Under 38.10 mm (1.500 in.)	GT125 GT185 GT250 GT380 GT550 GT750

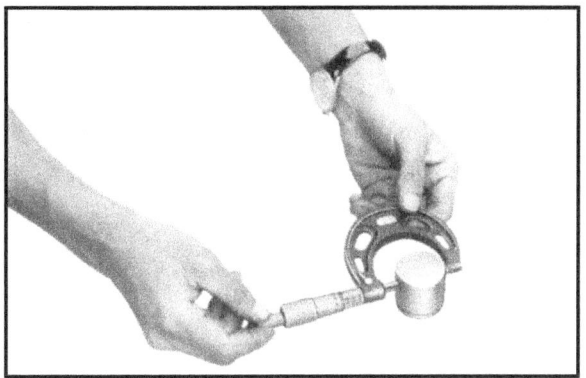

Fig. 4-4-7

3) Piston seal: No damage nor excessive wear
4) Piston boot: No damage nor settling
5) Pads Nos. 1 and 2: Not worn out of its limit (refer to "4-2-1 Inspecting of Pads").
6) Caliper body: No crack

4-4-5 Assembling

Follow the removal procedure in the reverse order. When assembling them, pay attention to the following points.
1) Apply "Suzuki Caliper Axle Grease" with property of high heat resistance onto the caliper axle.

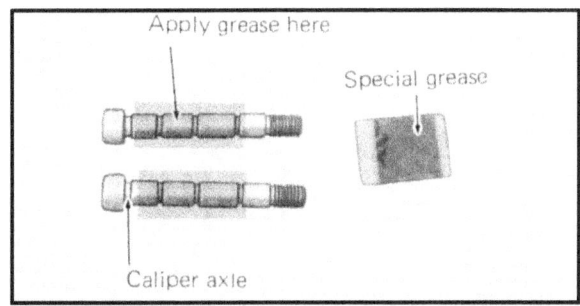

Fig. 4-4-8

2) Apply a generous amount of brake fluid onto the inner surface of the cylinder and periphery of the piston and then assemble.
3) Do not assemble the piston seal with it inclined or twisted. See Fig. 4-4-9.

4) In installing the piston, push it slowly into the cylinder while taking care not to damage the piston seal.

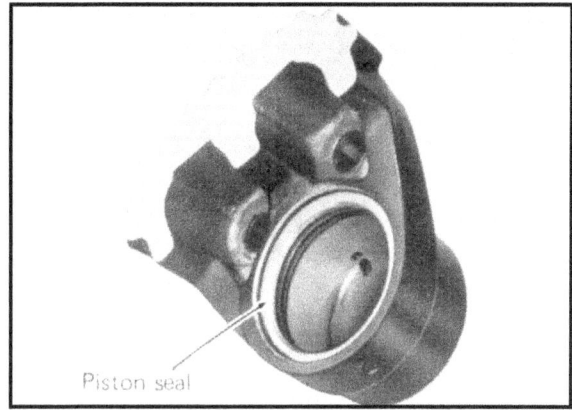

Fig. 4-4-9

5) Apply "Suzuki Brake Pad Grease" shown in Fig. 4-4-10 onto the periphery of pad No. 1 (refer to "4-2-2 Replacing of Pads").

Fig. 4-4-10

6) Bleed air after assembling (refer to "4-1-2 Air bleeding from brake system").
7) After bleeding air, check for brake fluid leakage while holding the brake lever tightly.
8) After a test run, check the pads and brake disc do not press each other excessively by turning the front wheel by hand.

4-5 Brake Disc

4-5-1 General
The brake disc, made of stainless steel having excellent heat-resistance and abrasion-proof properties, is fastened to the front hub with six high tensile strength bolts.

4-5-2 Checking

1) Runout of the brake disc should not be greater than the limit. Measure brake disc runout with a dial indicator as shown in Fig. 4-5-1. If the runout is over the limit on the largest periphery of the disc plate, check whether the cause lies in the front wheel bearing or the brake disc itself, and replace defective parts.

Standard	Limit	Model
0.1 mm (0.004 in.)	0.3 mm (0.012 in.)	GT125 GT185 GT250 GT380 GT550 GT750

Fig. 4-5-2

Fig. 4-5-1

2) Thickness of the brake disc should not be less than the limit. Measure its worn portion with a micrometer as shown in Fig. 4-5-2 and replace the brake disc if the thickness is less than the limit.

Standard	Limit	Model
5.00 mm (0.197 in.)	Under 4.00 mm (0.157 in.)	GT125 GT185
7.00 mm (0.276 in.)	Under 6.00 mm (0.236 in.)	GT250 GT380 GT550 GT750

3) Surface of the brake disc should be free from oil. Take care that no oil is adhered on the brake disc surface, since oil adhesion there is very dangerous. If oil is placed on the disc by mistake, wipe off the oil with a soft waste-cloth soaked with alcohol.

4) The brake disc fitting bolts should be securely tightened to the specified torque and should be secured with lock washers.

Fig. 4-5-3

4-6 Periodic Replacement Parts

The component parts of the master cylinder assembly and the caliper assembly may be worn and deteriorated in function in long period of use. However, it is generally difficult to foresee how long each component will further work with proper function thereafter, since deterioration of function much depends upon usage of brake by individual motorcycle.

Then, from safety points of view, the following is defined as periodic replacement parts in order to prevent unforeseen trouble caused by wearing of component.

Replace all the following parts at a time with Suzuki genuine parts sets.

Exchange interval: Two years

1. Components of master cylinder assembly
   (Use Suzuki Genuine parts: Master cylinder cup set)

   1. Primary cup
   2. Spring
   3. Piston
   4. Check valve
   5. Circlip
   6. Boot plate
   7. Boot
   8. Stop plate
   9. Boot stopper

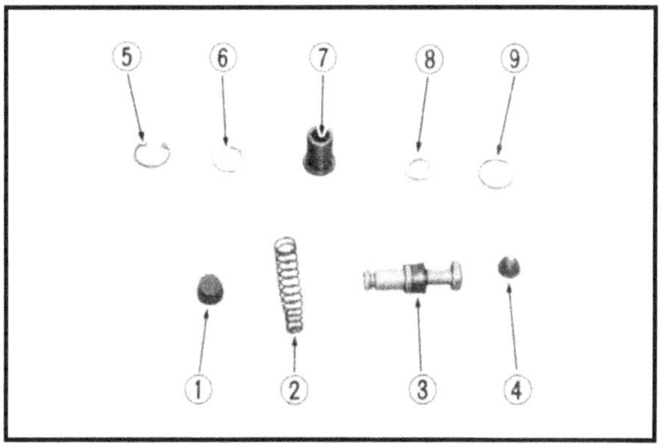

   Fig. 4-6-1

2. Component of caliper assembly
   (Use Suzuki Genuine parts: Pad and piston set)

   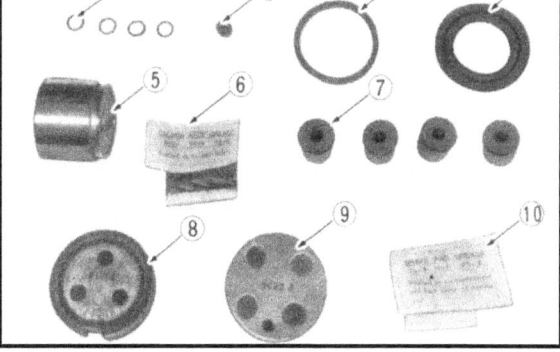

   1. "O" ring
   2. Stopper
   3. Piston seal
   4. Boot
   5. Piston
   6. Suzuki Caliper Axle Grease
   7. Axle shaft dust cover
   8. Pad No. 1
   9. Pad No. 2
   10. Suzuki Brake Pad Grease

   Fig. 4-6-2

Note: Pad and piston set includes two kinds of grease packed in pouch. Grease in the pouch printed "Caliper Axle Grease" should be used for the caliper axle and printed "Brake Pad Grease" for the pad No. 1.

Caution: Be sure to wash all component parts in the above sets with clean brake fluid before installing them into the master cylinder or caliper.

5. TIGHTENING TORQUE

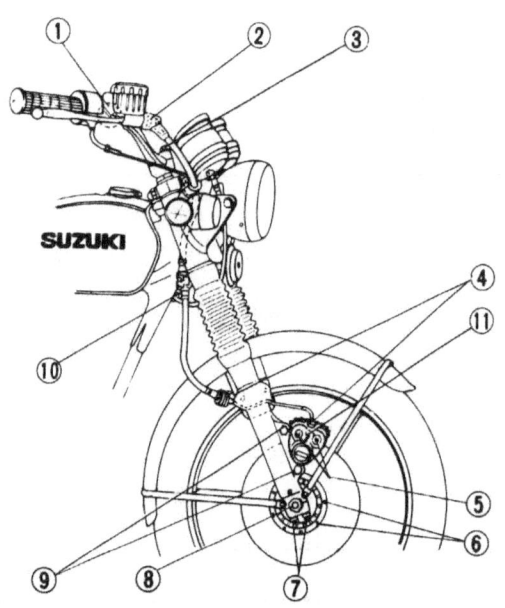
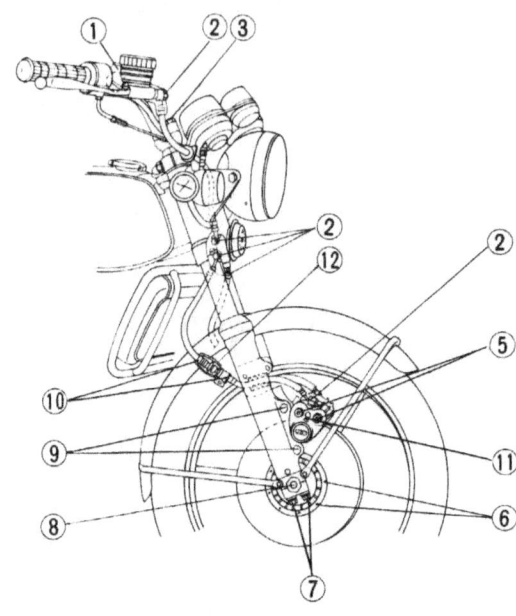

Fig. 5-1-1   Fig. 5-1-2

Item No.	Description	Bolt-and nut diameter mm	Tightening torque kg-cm	Tightening torque ft-lb
1	Master cylinder clamp bolt	6	50 to 80	3.6 to 5.8
2	Union bolt	10	150 to 250	11 to 18
3	Handlebar clamp bolt	8	120 to 200	9 to 14
4	Brake pipe nut	10	130 to 180	9.5 to 13
5	Caliper axle bolt	10	250 to 350	18 to 25
6	Brake disc fitting bolt	8	150 to 250	11 to 18
7	Front axle holder nut	8	150 to 250	11 to 18
8	Front axle shaft nut	12	360 to 520	26 to 38
9	Caliper fitting bolt	10	250 to 400	18 to 29
10	Brake hose joint	10	250 to 350	18 to 25
11	Bleeder bolt	7	60 to 90	4.3 to 6.5
12	Adaptor	10	250 to 300	18 to 22

6. SPECIAL TOOLS FOR DISC BRAKE

6-1 Special tools

The following special tools are necessary for disassembling and reassembling disc brakes. Please use these special tools to ensure your operation.

Part No.	Description	Used for
09920-73110	Special circlip opener	Disassembling master cylinder
09900-06904	8 mm hexagon L-type wrench	Disassembling caliper

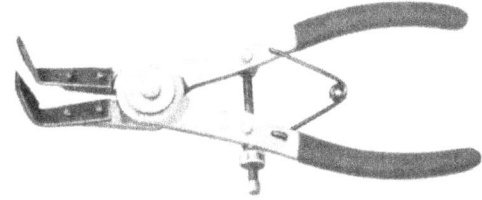

Special circlip opener   Fig. 6-1-1

8 mm hexagon L-type wrench   Fig. 6-1-2

6-2 Necessary materials

The two types of grease shown in the following table are applied to the moving parts when overhauling the disc brake. These grease feature their high lubrication and pressure withstanding performances even at a high temperature, and further, they do not affect rubber parts. When overhauling the disc brake, do not use other grease but these two types only.

Part No.	Description	Use
99000-25100	Suzuki brake pad grease	Lubrication of pad No.1
99000-25110	Suzuki caliper axle grease	Lubrication of caliper axle

Suzuki brake pad grease   Fig. 6-2-1

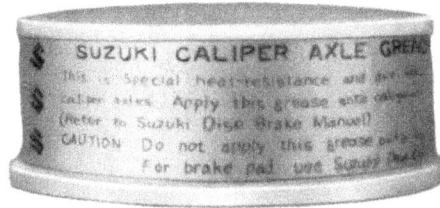

Suzuki caliper axle grease   Fig. 6-2-2

SUZUKI MOTOR CO., LTD.

SUZUKI SERVICE MANUAL

MODEL

VM24SC CARBURETOR

FOREWORD

This manual is published for the information and use of the personnel who are concerned in the maintenance of the VM24SC and VM28SC Carburetors used on the 1974 Suzuki GT380L and GT550L. The manual applies only to the carburetors and is prepared for use with the manuals published for the motorcycles.

It has its own index and contains a description of the major components and their functions as well as maintenance.

All information, illustrations and specifications contained in this manual are based on the products manufactured before Nov., 1974. Any changes, deletions or additions to this manual will be followed by the Service Bulletin.

Feb., 1974

SUZUKI MOTOR CO., LTD.

INDEX

SUZUKI TYPE VM CARBURETOR FOR GT380 & GT550

CHAPTER 1. DESCRIPTION 1
    1. Operation 2
    2. Specifications 7
    3. Troubleshooting Guide 7
    4. Special Tools, Adhesive and Grease 8

CHAPTER 2. REPAIR AND ADJUSTMENT 9
    1. Disassembly 9
    2. Inspections 11
    3. Assembly and Adjustment 12
    4. Carburetor Adjustment 18

CHAPTER 1. DESCRIPTION

The Model VM24SC and VM28SC Carburetors currently used on the Suzuki GT380L and GT550L are of an AMAL type carburetor with an independent starting circuit. It also includes an additional system of linkage to force the throttle valve to the closed position to provide for sticky valve or broken valve return spring.

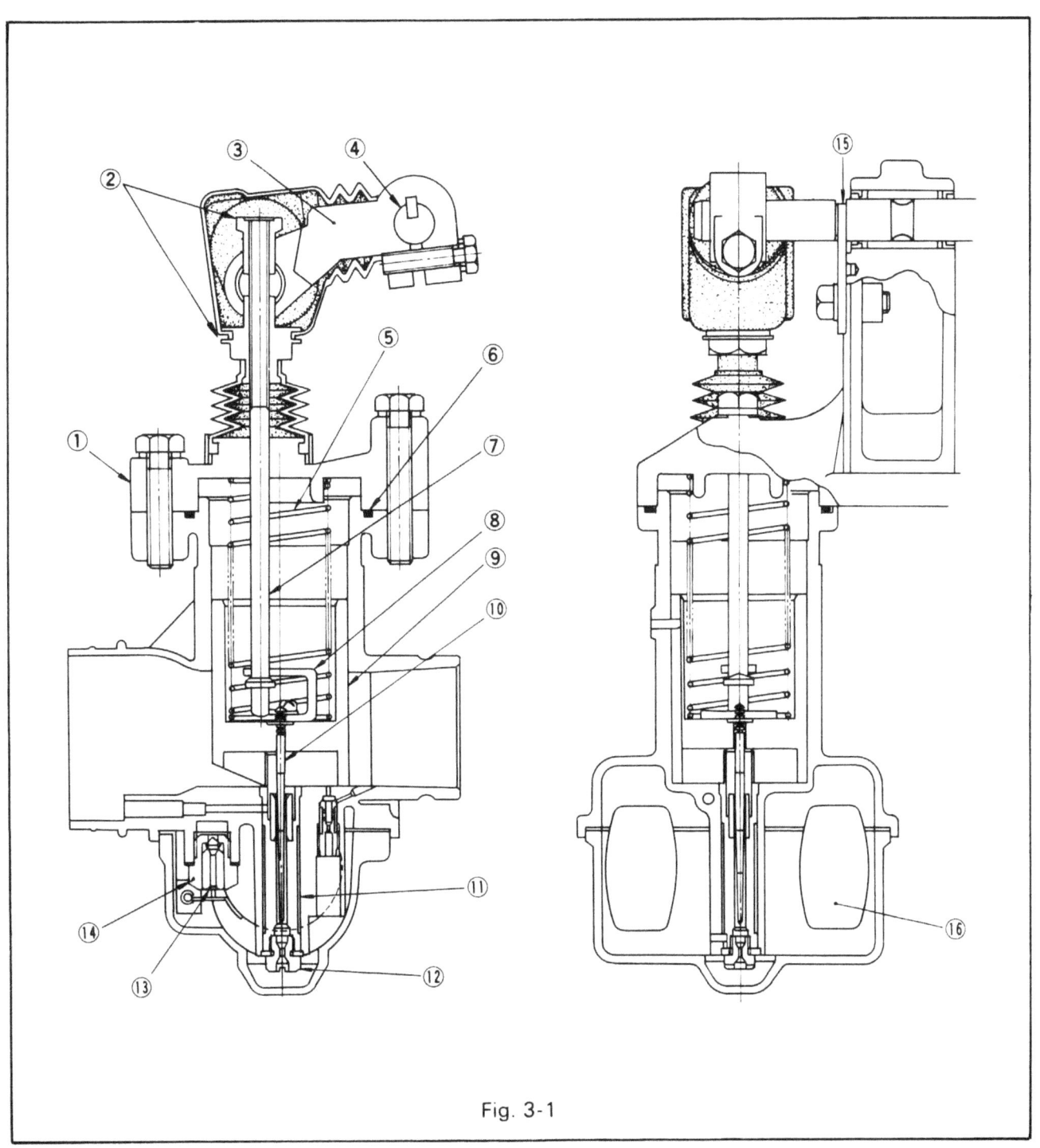

Fig. 3-1

1. Mixing chamber top
2. Throttle valve adjust nut
3. Throttle valve arm
4. Throttle valve shaft
5. Throttle valve spring
6. O-ring
7. Throttle valve rod
8. Jet needle set plate
9. Throttle valve
10. Jet needle
11. Needle jet
12. Main jet
13. Needle valve
14. Valve seat
15. Shaft stop plate
16. Float

1. Operation

a) Forced throttle-return system

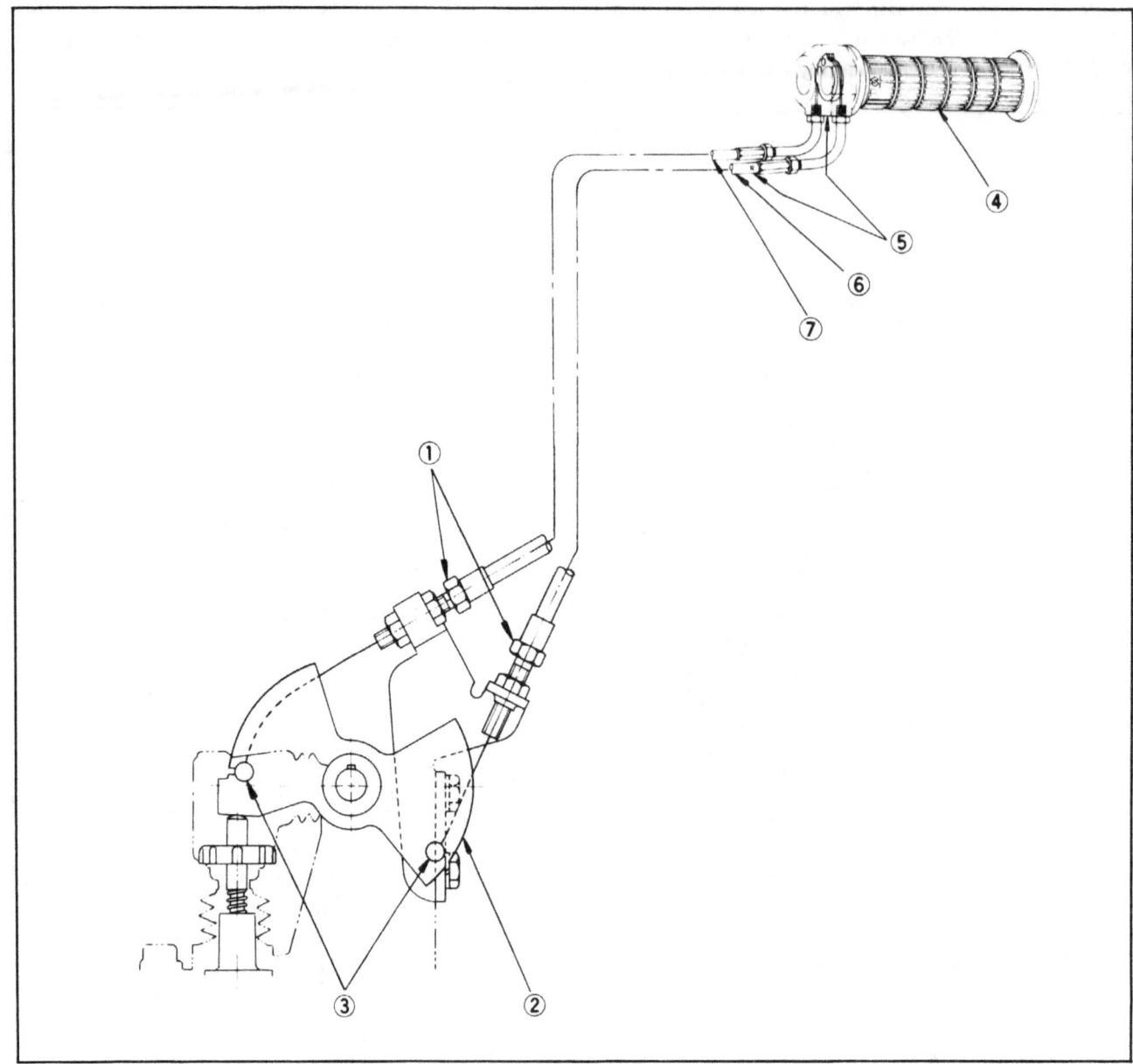

Fig. 3-2

1. Throttle cable adjuster
2. Pulley
3. Cable end
4. Throttle grip
5. Identification letter "R" (return side)
6. Throttle cable (return side)
7. Throttle cable (pull side)

The forced throttle-return system provides an added means of returning the throttle valve to the closed position. Fig. 1 shows an exaggerated view of the system to understand the operation that takes place when the system is operated.

When the throttle grip is turned inward, the pulley is pulled up by a cable; i.e., the throttle is opened.

Now, when the grip is twisted outward, a spring produces some further closing of the throttle valve and spring-loads it in the closed position.

The system forces the throttle valve toward the closed position even when the valve has stuck or the spring has been broken.

2

b) Slow system

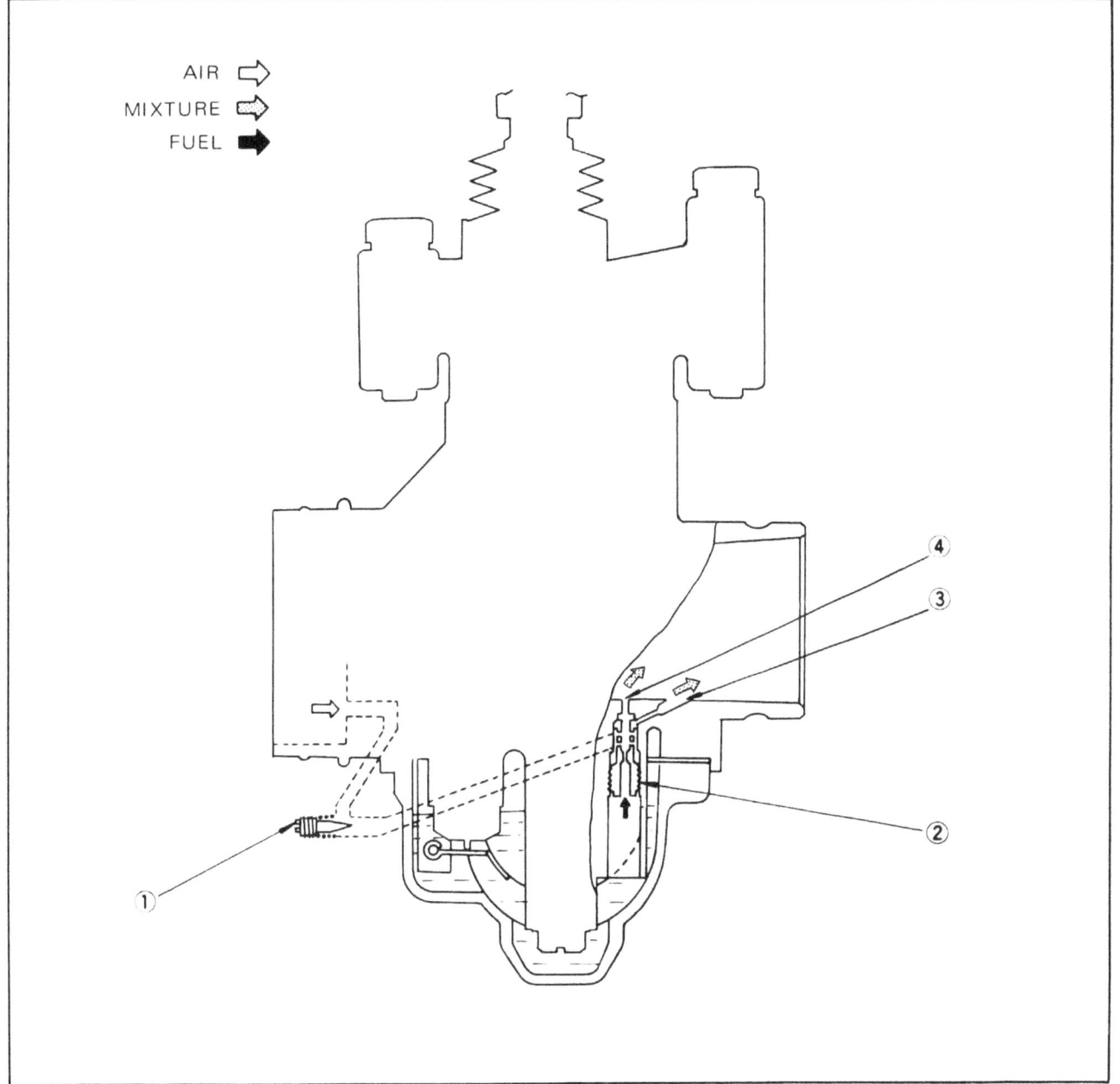

Fig. 3-3

1. Pilot air screw
2. Pilot jet
3. Bypass
4. Pilot outlet

When the throttle valve is closed or only slightly opened, the speed of air flowing through the air horn is low. As a result, there will be very little vacuum at the venturi to draw fuel from the needle jet. The slow system supplies fuel during operation with the throttle closed or almost closed.
The fuel from the float chamber is first metered by the pilot jet, where it mixes with air passing by the pilot air screw. The resultant mixture will then discharge out into the carburetor air horn through the pilot outlet and bypass port where it is to be mixed with the main incoming air stream passing through the throttle valve.

c) Main system

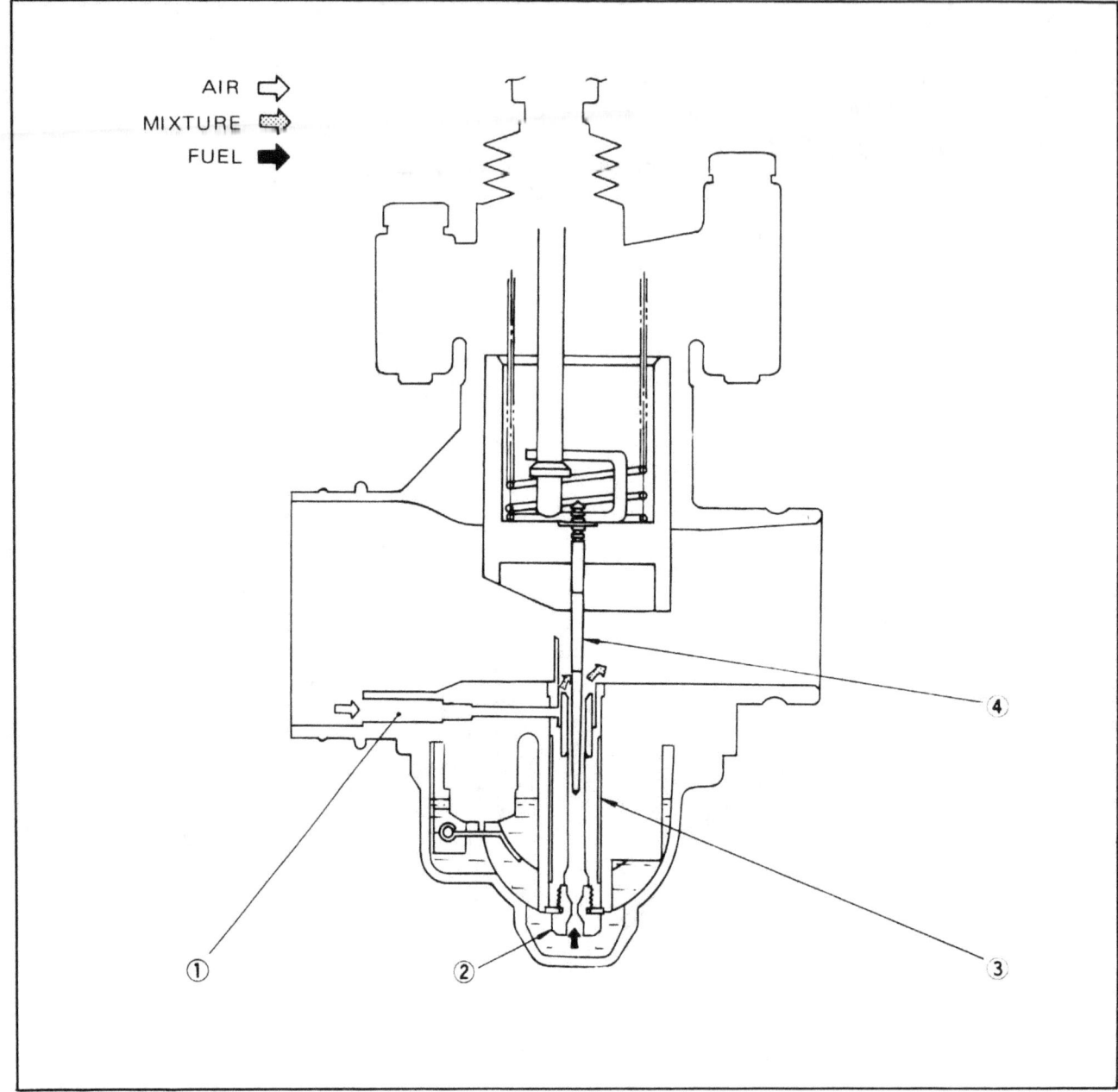

Fig. 3-4

1. Main air passage
2. Main jet
3. Needle jet
4. Jet needle

When the throttle is opened, the fuel in the float chamber is subject to strong engine suction since the vacuum at the venturi is increased.

The fuel in the float chamber is then metered by the main jet as it passes through it. The fuel is again metered by the clearance between the needle jet and jet needle, being mixed with air flowing from the main air passage. The mixture will then be discharged into the carburetor venturi. At the venturi, the mixture meets another air flowing from the main bore, being drawn into the engine.

The fuel is given correct mixture proportions as it passes through the needle jet since the effective size of the needle jet depends on the throttle position.

d) Starter system

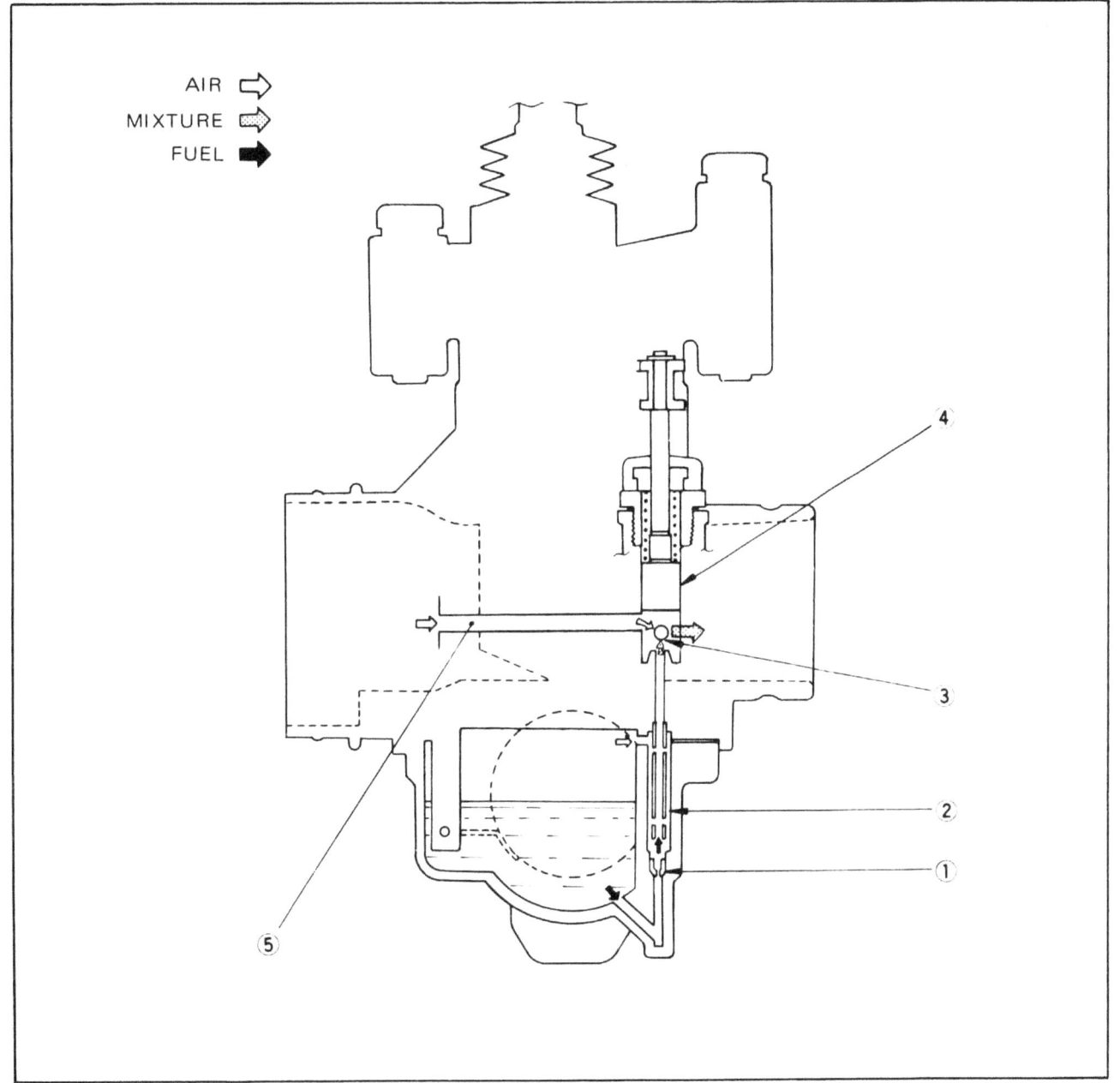

Fig. 3-5

1. Starter jet
2. Starter pipe
3. Starter outlet
4. Starter plunger
5. Starter air passage

When the choke lever at the left side of the carburetor is pulled up, the starter plungers are pushed up by the starter rod. The action allows the fuel to bleed into the starter circuit.

The starter jet is supplied with fuel directly from the float chamber. The fuel is first metered by the starter jet as it passes through it. The metered fuel then goes up into the starter pipe where it enters air from the float chamber.

This rich mixture meets air flowing from the starter air passage when it reaches the starter plunger chamber and is discharged through the starter outlet into the engine directly.

The right side carburetor receives the mixture from the starter system of the main carburetor through a pipe.

e) Float system

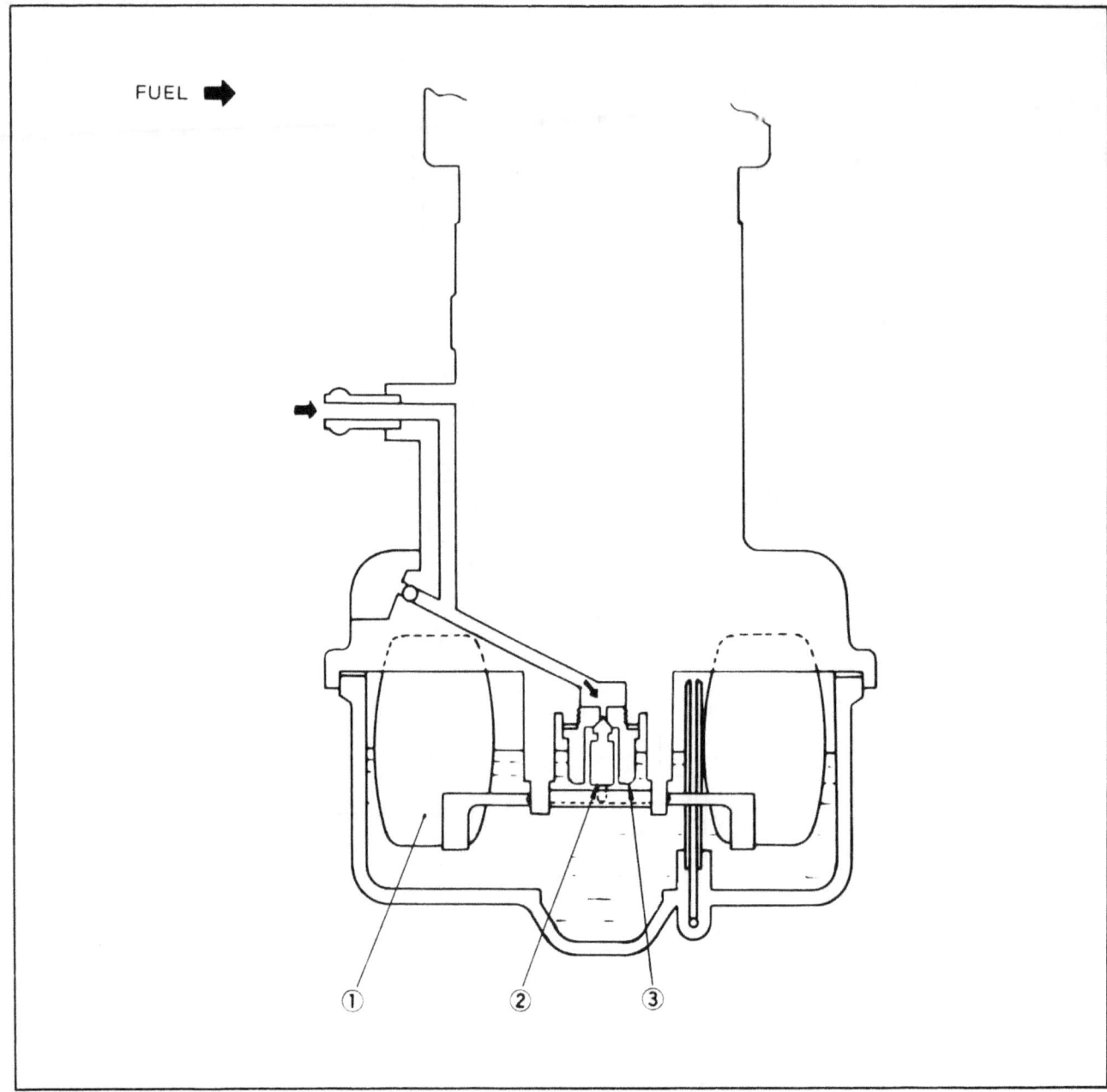

Fig. 3-6

1. Float
2. Needle valve
3. Valve seat

The float system consists of float, needle valve and valve seat, assembled to maintain a constant level of fuel in the float chamber. When fuel enters the float chamber, this causes the float to move up. The valve is so designed that, if the float moves up, it is pushed up into the valve seat. This shuts off the fuel inlet so that no fuel can enter.
If the float level lowers, the float moves down; i.e., fuel can now enter since this releases the needle valve.
The same sequence of events takes place to maintain a constant level of fuel in the float chamber.

2. Specifications

		GT380	GT550
Type		VM24SC	VM28SC
Bore Size		24 mm	28 mm
Main Jet	R & L	#80	#97.5
	C	#80	#95
Jet Needle		4DH7-2nd	5DH21-4th
Needle Jet		O-2	P-0
Cutaway		3.0	2.5
Bypass		1.4 mm	1.4 mm
Pilot Outlet		0.8 mm	0.8 mm
Air Screw Opening		1 ¼	1 ½
Valve Seat		2.0 mm	2.0 mm
Starter Jet		#80	#90
Bypass		3.75 mm	5.15 mm
Float Level		25.75 mm	25.75 mm
Identification Mark		33110 R,M,L	34110 R,M,L

3. Troubleshooting Guide

Symptom	Probable Cause	Remedy
Rough idling or slow speed	1. Clogged pilot jet or loose pilot jet	Clean and retighten
	2. Leaky float chamber gasket	Retighten. If necessary, replace gasket
	3. Carburetor out of adjustment	Adjust
	4. Improper float level	Adjust. Check needle valve and float and, if necessary, replace
	5. Pilot air screw out of adjustment	Adjust
	6. Clogged bypass and pilot outlet	Clean
Improper part- and full-throttle operation	1. Clogged main jet	Clean or retighten
	2. Carburetor out of adjustment	Adjust
	3. Improper float level	Adjust. Check needle valve and float and, if necessary, replace
Hard starting (with choke lever in operation)	1. Improper throttle valve opening	Adjust
	2. Clogged starter jet	Clean
	3. Starter plunger out of order	Retighten starter rod screw

4. Special Tools, Adhesive and Grease

a) Throttle valve adjust tool
This tool is designed to adjust carburetor without removing it from the motorcycle. It is a combination of a 10 mm box wrench and plain head screwdriver.

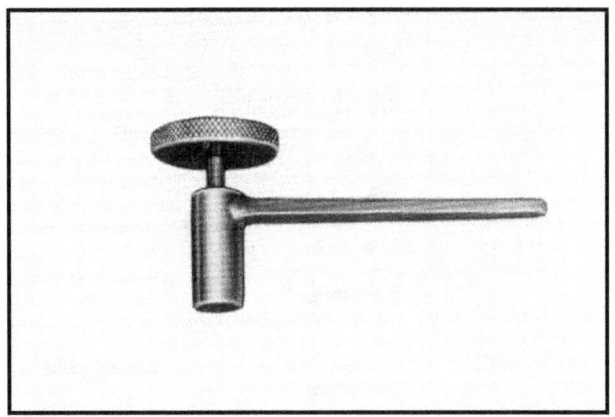

Fig. 3-6

Part Name	Throttle Valve Adjust Screw
Part No.	09913-13110

b) Thread lock cement

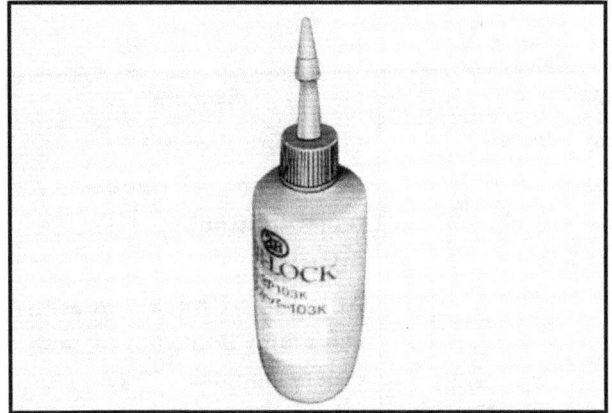

Fig. 3-7

Part Name	Thread Lock Cement "103K"
Part No.	99000-32030

The thread lock cement is used to lock the starter rod screw.

c) Grease

Fig. 3-8

Part Name	Suzuki Super Grease "C"
Part No.	99000-25030

Suzuki Super Grease "C" is used to lubricate the throttle valve rod and throttle valve arm.

CHAPTER 2. REPAIR AND ADJUSTMENT

1. Disassembly

a) Remove the fuel and vacuum hoses; take out the fuel tank. Remove the air cleaner.

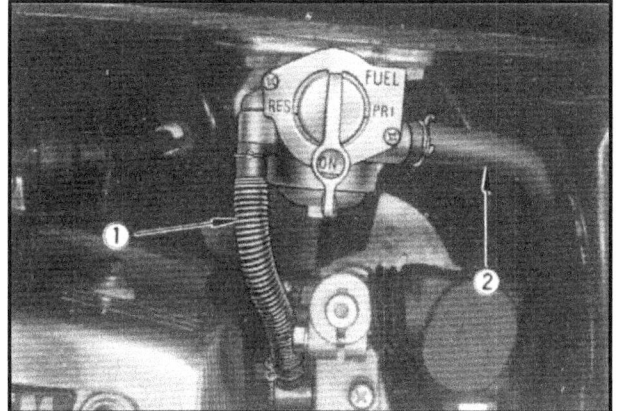

1. Vacuum hose   2. Fuel hose   Fig. 4-1

b) Loosen the throttle cable adjuster and disconnect the cable end from the pulley.

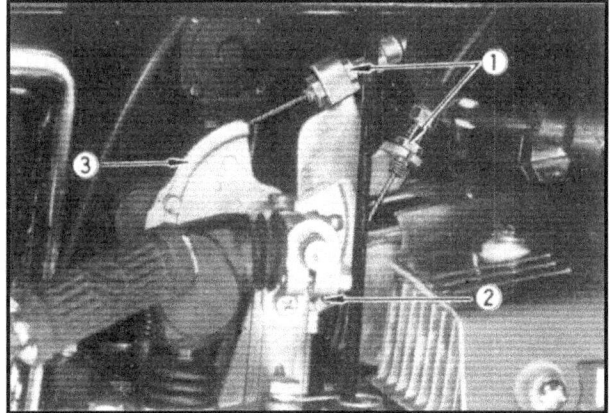

1. Throttle cable adjuster   3. Pulley   Fig. 4-2
2. Cable end

c) Loosen the clamp at the carburetor inlet and take out the carburetor.

d) Unscrew screw securing the choke lever in place to the carburetor.
Be careful when removing the lever since the steel ball is spring-loaded. Loosen the starter rod screws and pull off the starter rod.

1. Choke lever   3. Starter rod   Fig. 4-3
2. Choke lever screw   4. Starter rod screw

e) Remove the mixing chamber top complete with the throttle valve.

f) Remove the boot; loosen and upper and lower throttle valve adjust nuts. Separate the throttle valve from the chamber.

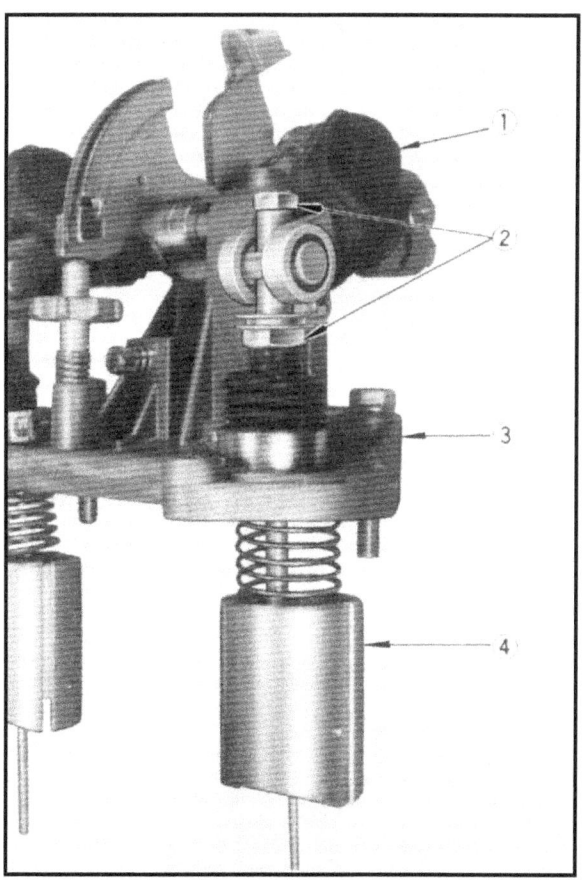

Fig. 4-4
1. Boot   3. Mixing chamber top
2. Throttle valve adjust nut   4. Throttle valve

g) Loosen the jet needle set plate screw inside the throttle valve.

j) Remove the float chamber; take out the main and pilot jets.

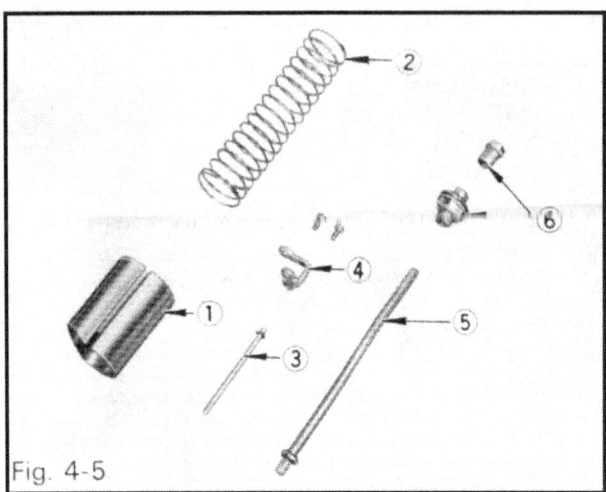

Fig. 4-5

1. Throttle valve
2. Throttle valve spring
3. Jet needle
4. Jet needle set plate
5. Throttle valve rod
6. Throttle valve adjust nut

h) Unscrew bolts securing the throttle valve arm and pulley in place; back off the throttle valve shaft stopper screw.

1. Main jet
2. Pilot jet
Fig. 4-8

k) Remove the main jet washer. Carefully drive out the needle jet toward the mixing chamber by tapping it on the bottom.

1. Throttle valve arm
2. Throttle valve shaft
3. Throttle valve shaft stopper
4. Pulley
Fig. 4-6

i) Pry off the woodruff key from the keyway in the throttle valve shaft while moving the pulley and throttle valve arm right and left. Remove shaft from the mixing chamber top.

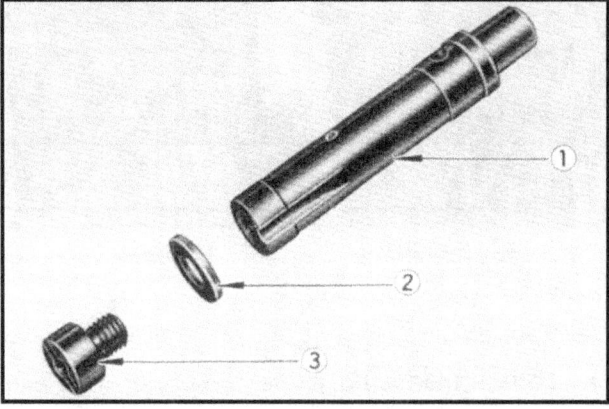

1. Needle jet
2. Main jet washer
3. Main jet
Fig. 4-9

1. Woodruff key
2. Throttle valve shaft
Fig. 4-7

2. Inspections

a) Throttle valve

Examine the throttle valve, and make sure that it is in good condition, particularly on its sliding surface.
Replace the carburetor as an assembled unit if the valve is scored or stepped excessively.

b) Needle valve and valve seat

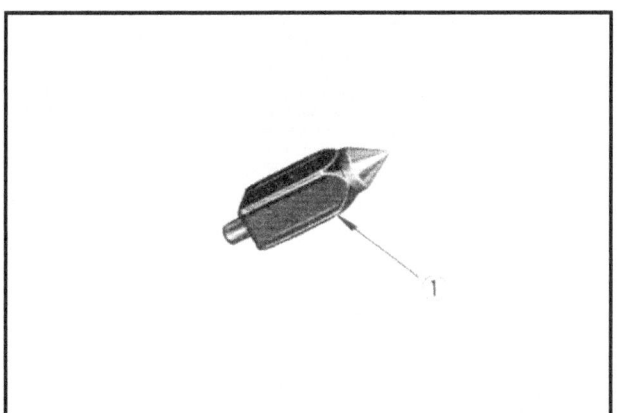

1. Needle valve   Fig. 4-10

Check the tapered point of the needle valve to see if it is not worn. If otherwise, replace the needle valve and valve seat as a set.

c) Float level

A Float height   Fig. 4-11

Remove the float chamber and gasket. With the carburetor tilted at 10-30° from vertical, measure the distance from the gasket surface and top of the float. Adjustment can be made by bending the float arm as necessary.

Standard float height	25.75 ± 1 mm (1.01 ± 0.04 in)

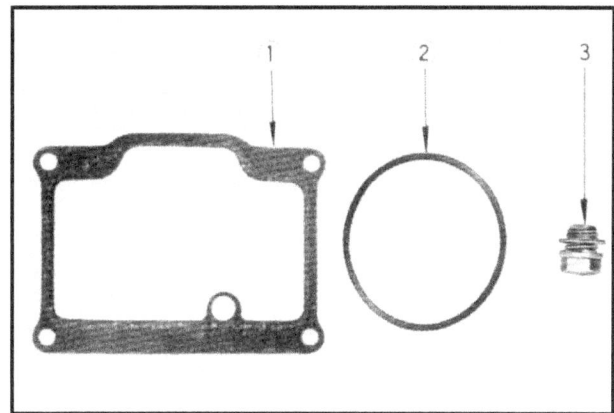

1. Float chamber gasket   3. Valve seat gasket
2. Mixing chamber top O-ring

Fig. 4-12

Check the float chamber gasket, mixing chamber O-ring and valve seat to be certain that these are not broken or weakened. If otherwise, discard the old ones and install new ones.

3. Assembly and Adjustment

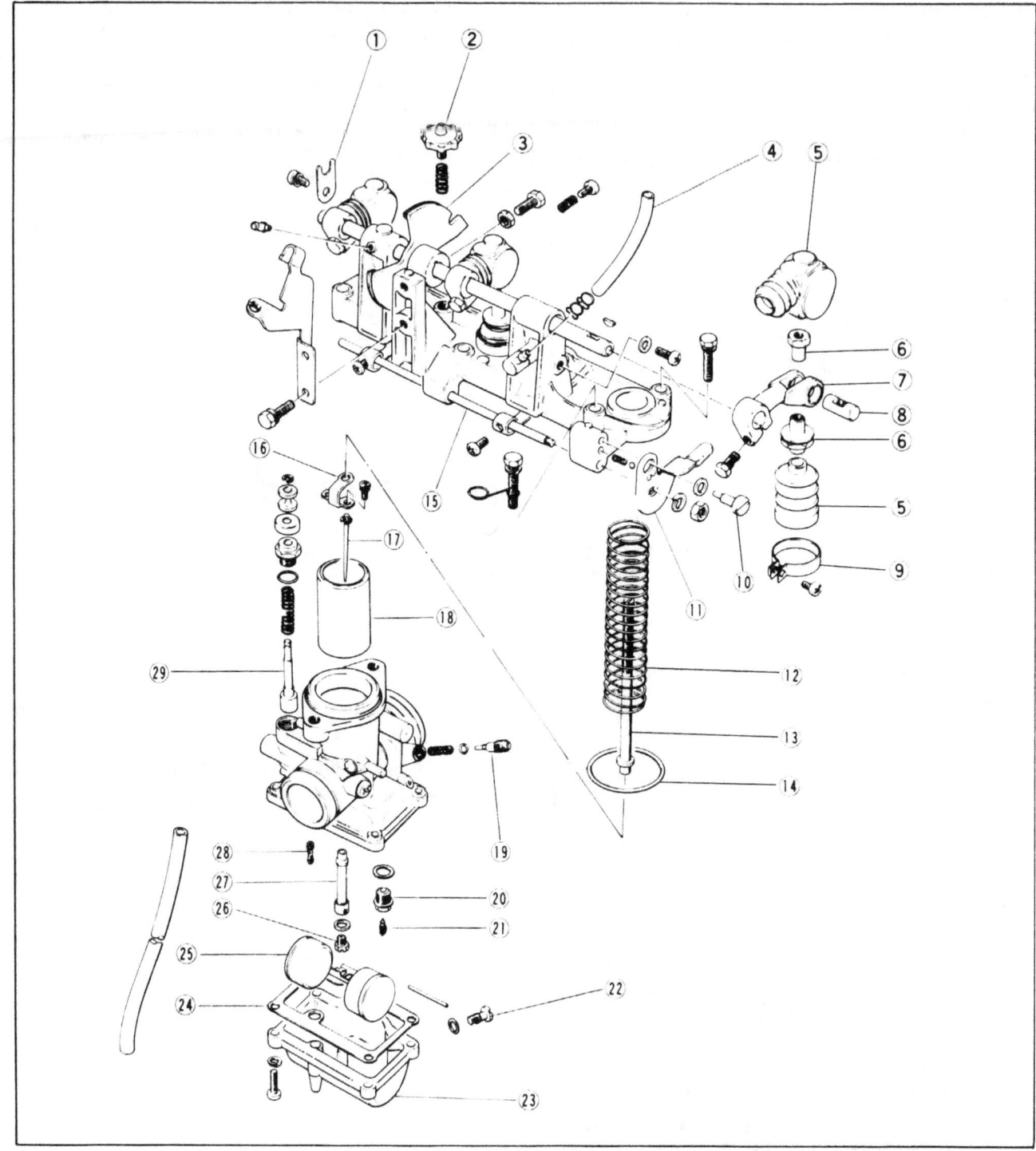

Fig. 4-13

1. Throttle valve shaft stopper
2. Throttle valve stop screw
3. Pulley
4. Vacuum hose
5. Boot
6. Throttle valve adjust nut
7. Throttle valve arm
8. Arm shaft
9. Clamp
10. Choke lever screw
11. Choke lever
12. Throttle valve spring
13. Throttle valve rod
14. Mixing chamber top O-ring
15. Starter rod
16. Jet needle set plate
17. Jet needle
18. Throttle valve
19. Pilot air screw
20. Valve seat
21. Needle valve
22. Drain plug
23. Float chamber
24. Float chamber gasket
25. Float
26. Main jet
27. Needle jet
28. Pilot jet
29. Starter plunger

Wash all parts in clean solvent and dry with compressed air.

a) Reaching from the mixing chamber side, install the needle jet in place.

Make sure that the needle jet groove aligns with the needle jet holder dowel pin.

1. Dowel pin   2. Needle jet holder   Fig. 4-14

b) Install the main and pilot jets in their respective positions.
c) Install the needle valve and float; place the float chamber in position.
d) Install the jet needle in the throttle valve; assemble the needle valve set plate and throttle valve rod with the throttle valve.
e) Position the pulley between the right mixing chamber top column and throttle cable bracket. Run the throttle valve shaft through the right column, pulley, throttle valve arm and left column.

Note:

Install the mixing chamber bolts before installing the throttle valve arm. If this caution is neglected, the bolt cannot be installed.

1. Throttle valve shaft   4. Mixing chamber top column
2. Throttle cable bracket   5. Mixing chamber top bolt
3. Pulley   Fig. 4-15

f) Press three woodruff keys in to place in the keyways in the throttle valve shaft. Install the pulley, being careful that the groove in the pulley is lined with the keys. Align lug of the throttle valve shaft stopper and hole in the mixing chamber top column; secure the throttle valve shaft.

1. Wooderuff key   3. Throttle valve shaft stopper
2. Lug   Fig. 4-16

g) Pump "Suzuki Super Grease C" through the grease fitting at the top column until excess grease shows out on the throttle vale shaft.

1. Grease fitting   Fig. 4-17

h) Approximate the pulley so that the thicker area is in line with the throttle valve stop screws. Secure the pulley with the pulley bolt, being careful not to disturb the above setup.

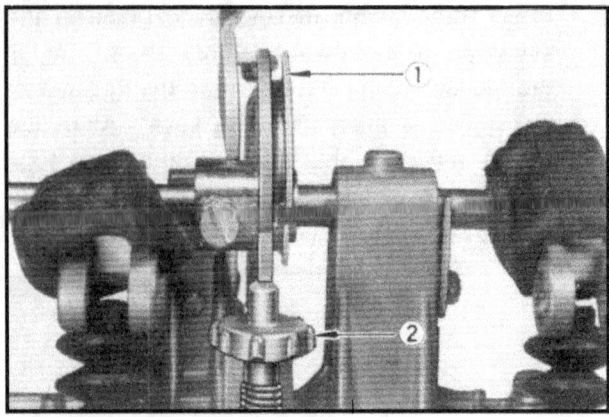

1. Pulley 2. Throttle valve stop screw Fig. 4-18

i) Apply a coating of "Suzuki Super Grease C" to the bearing surfaces of the throttle valve arm. Enter the throttle valve arm shaft through the holes in the arm.

1. Throttle valve arm shaft Fig. 4-19
2. Throttle valve arm

j) Enter the throttle valve into place in the carburetor body. Be sure to line up the groove in the valve with the dowel on the carburetor. Be extremely careful that the throttle valve be installed in the night side carburetor when it carries a marking (dent) on the left side of the groove as shown.

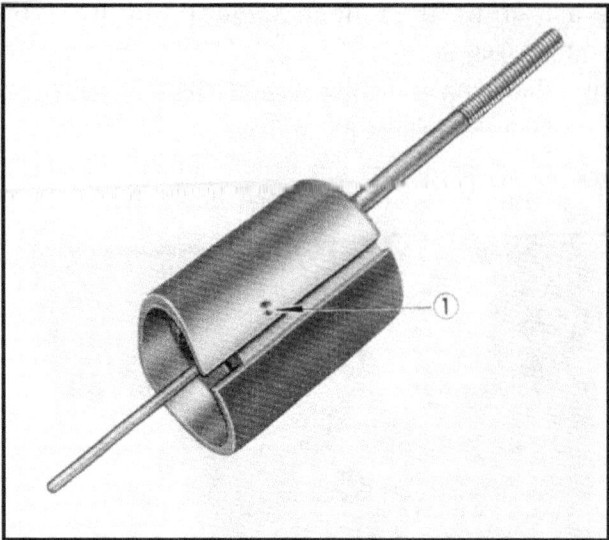

1. Dent mark Fig. 4-20

k) Put the mixing chamber top on the carburetor body and screw in the throttle valve adjust nut until the end of the throttle valve rod comes out from the nut slightly.

1. Throttle valve arm Fig. 4-21
2. Throttle valve adjust nut 3. Throttle valve rod

1) Tighten the throttle valve arm on the shaft with the arm bolt as per the instruction given in the accompanying sketch below.

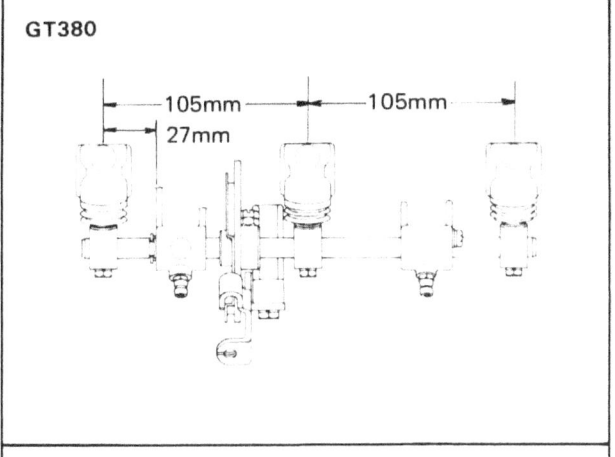

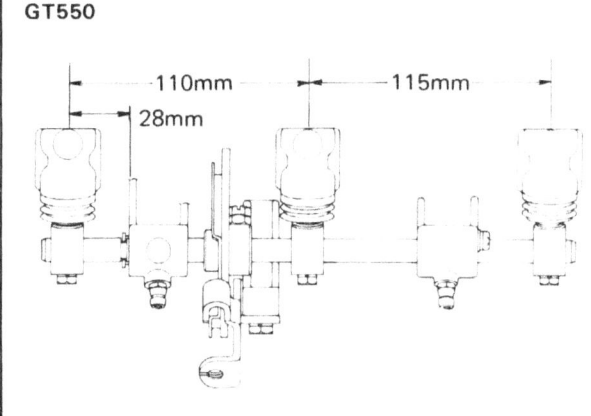

Fig. 4-22

After the above step has been completed, move the pulley several times to make sure that the arm is not interfering with the throttle valve adjust nut. If otherwise, relocate the arm on the shaft.

m) Turn in the throttle valve stop screw all the way until it bottoms; turn it out 1-1/2 turns. Without disturbing the above setup, turn the throttle adjust nut either in or out as necessary until the clearance between the lower end of the throttle valve and main bore is 0.8 ~ 1 mm (0.03 ~ 0.04 in) as viewed from the carburetor outlet (on each carburetor).

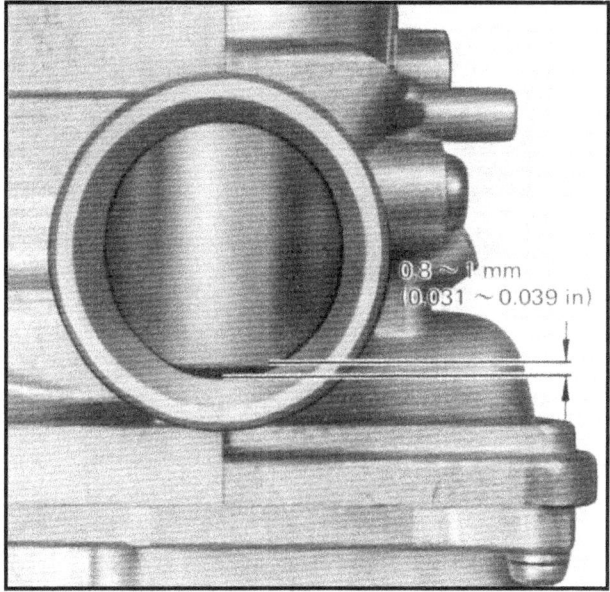

Fig. 4-23

n) Turn in or out the throttle valve full-open stop screw so that the lower end of the throttle valve is 0.5 ~ 1 mm (0.02 ~ 0.04 in) above the main bore as viewed from the carburetor inlet. Be sure to keep the throttle fully open during operation.

Fig. 4-24

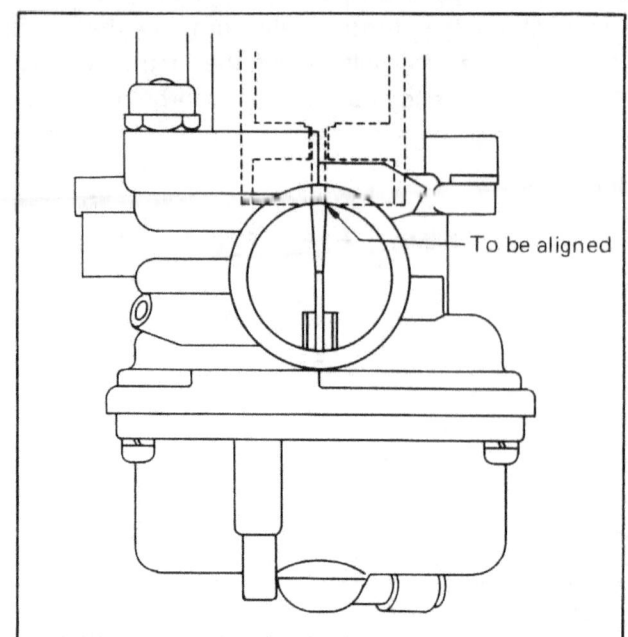

Fig. 4-26

1. Pulley
2. Throttle valve full-open stop screw
3. Throttle valve stop screw

Fig. 4-25

o) Hold any throttle valve so that it is in line with the edge of the main bore as viewed from the inlet. Using this valve as a reference, line up the remaining valves with throttle valve adjust nut. Tighten the throttle adjust nuts securely.

p) Assemble in the reverse order of the disassembly. Start and warm up the engine for about five minutes. Turn the throttle stop screw either in or out as necessary so that the engine will run approx. 1,100 rpm.

q) Adjust the throttle cables (pull side and return side) so that the deflections are 3 ~ 5 mm (0.12 ~ 0.20 in) when thumb pressure 100 ~ 200 g (0.22 ~ 0.44 lb) is applied at a point midway between the cable end and cable adjuster.

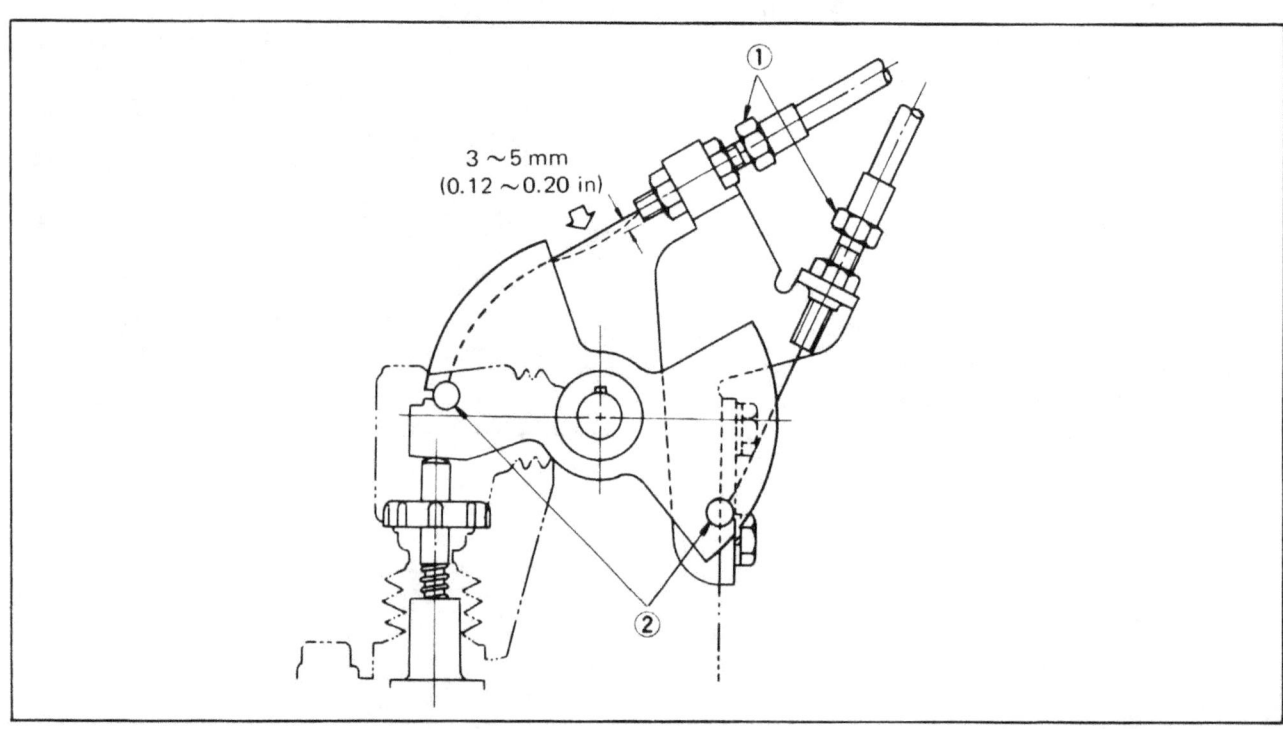

1. Throttle cable adjuster
2. Cable end

Fig. 4-27

r) Remove the plug screw from the right carburetor. Make sure that the marking on the oil pump control lever aligns with that on the oil pump when the dent mark is at the top edge of the vacant hole made by removing the plug screw. Adjustment can be made by turning the oil pump cable adjuster in or out as required.

1. Aligning mark
2. Oil pump cable adjuster
3. Dent mark

Fig. 4-28

4. Carburetor Adjustment

Observe either of the following procedures when it becomes necessary to make a throttle-opening (carburetor balance) adjustment during periodic maintenance service etc.

Off-motorcycle adjustment:
   Follow the steps "o" thru "h" under ASSEMBLY in Chapter 3.

On-motorcycle adjustment:
   Proper procedure for adjustment of carburetor on motorcycle is as follows. However, carburetor should not be adjusted unless the following items are properly adjusted.
   • Contact breaker point gap
   • Spark plug gap
   • Ignition timing
   • Pilot air screw opening
   • Throttle cable play

1. Start and warm up the engine for about five minutes.
2. Turn in the throttle valve stop screw so that the engine will run at approx. 1,500 rpm.
3. Ground the breaker point or remove the spark plug cap so that the right cylinder will not fire. Turn the center throttle valve adjust nut so that the engine will run at 1,000 rpm. Use tool "Throttle Valve Adjust Tool No. 09913-13110" to turn the adjust nut and screw.

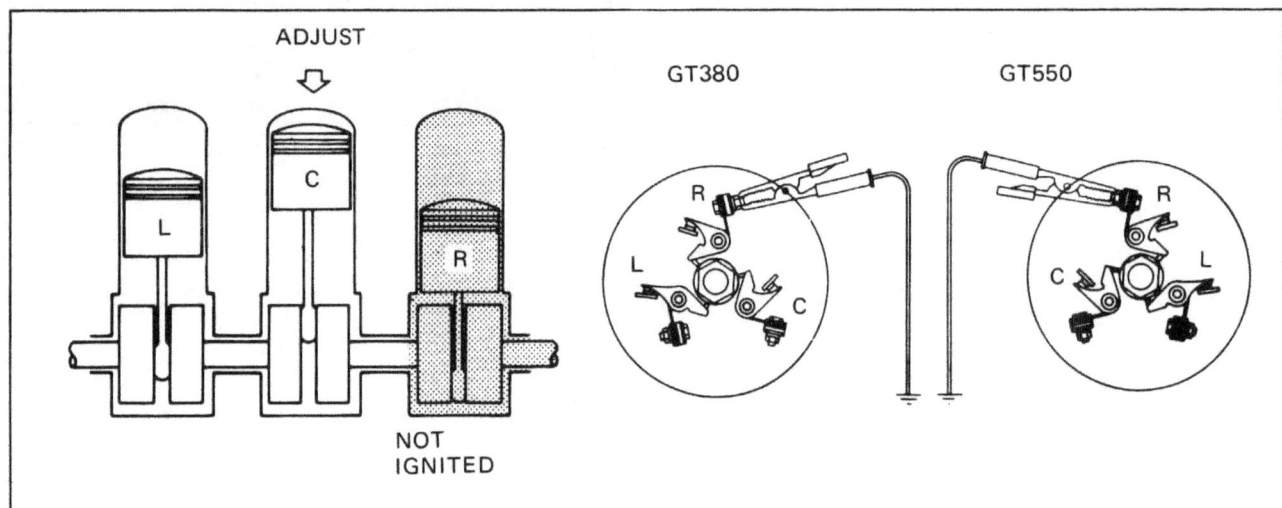

4. In like manner as above, disable the center cylinder. Adjust the engine speed to 1,000 rpm by means of the right carburetor throttle valve adjust nut.

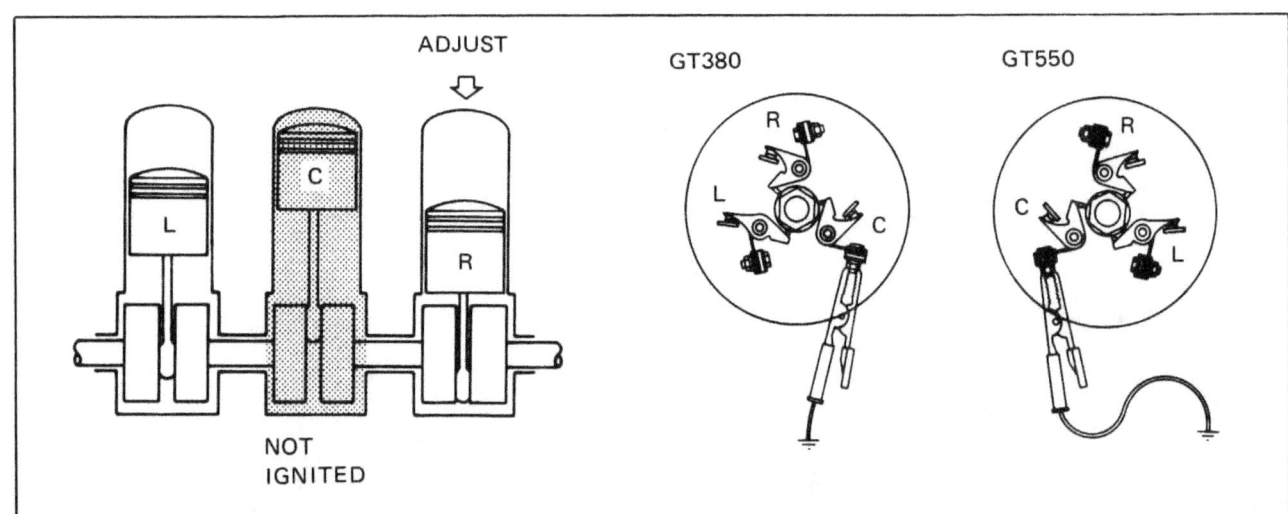

5. Disable the left cylinder. Read the engine speed.

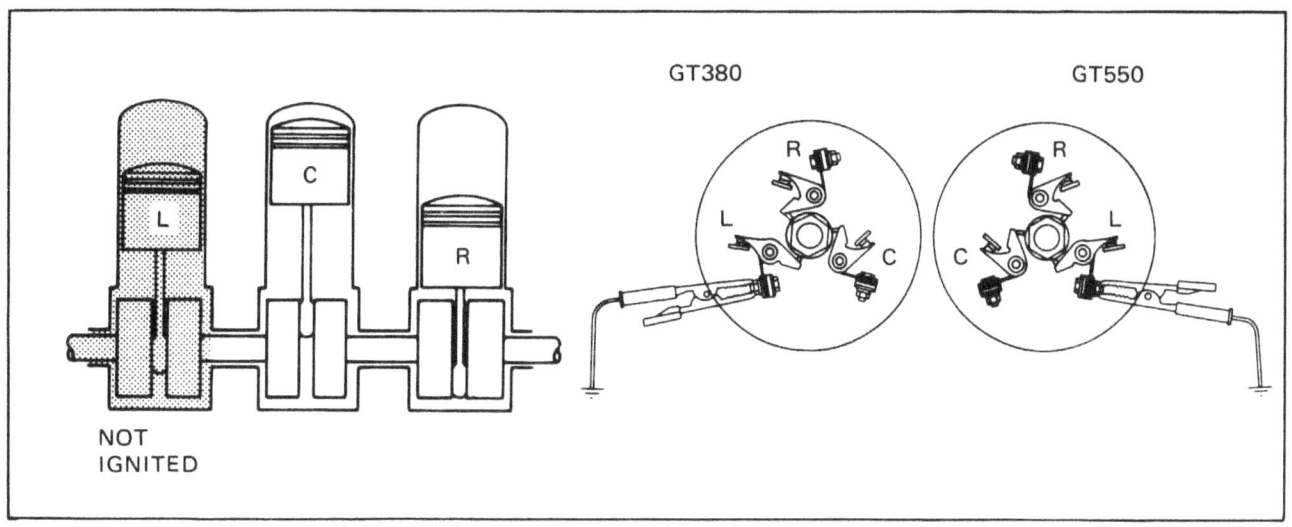

6. Disable the right cylinder. Rotate the left carburetor throttle valve adjust nut so that the engine will run at the same speed as that taken in Step (5) above.

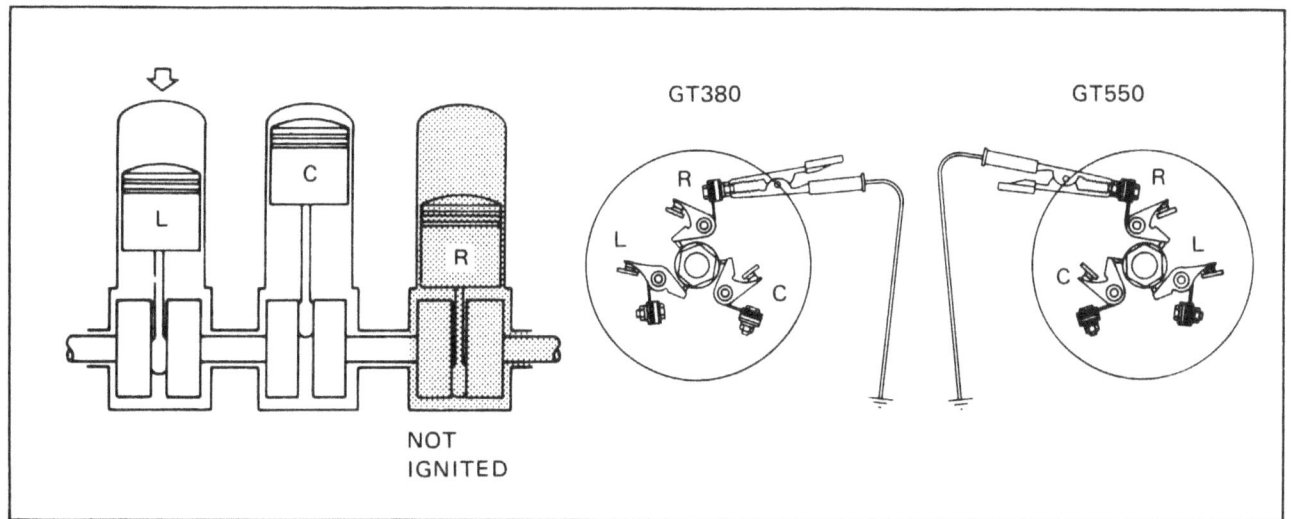

7. Finally, fire all cylinders. Turn out the throttle stop screw so that the engine will run at 1,100 rpm.

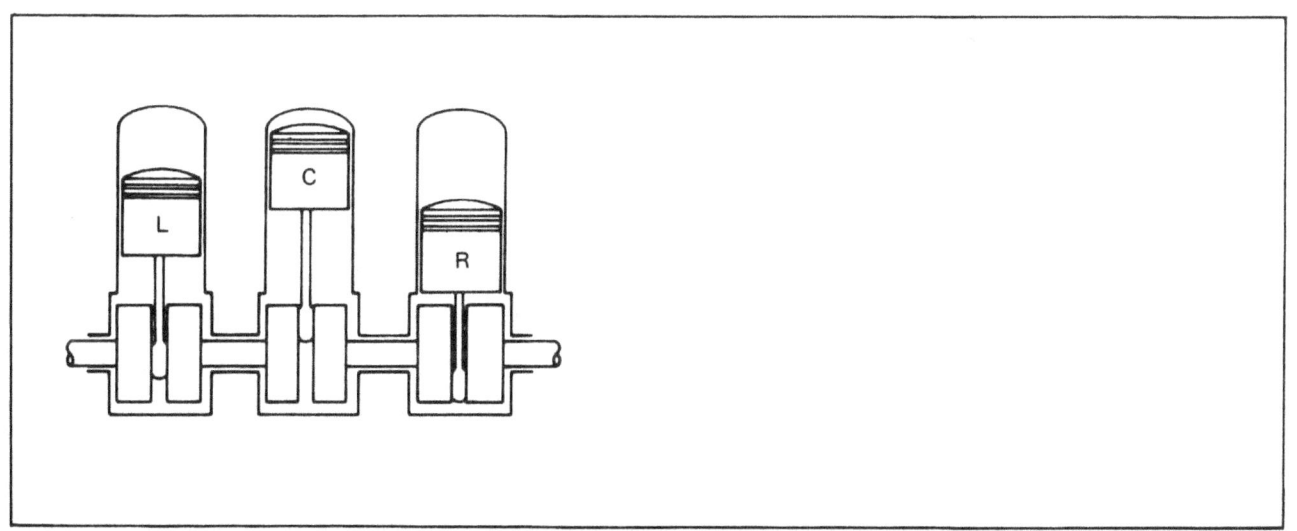

SUZUKI MOTOR CO., LTD.

VELOCEPRESS.com - MOTORCYCLE MANUALS BY MAKE

AJS 1932-1948 SINGLES & TWINS 250cc THRU 1000cc (BOOK OF)
AJS 1945-1956 SINGLES RIGID & SPTRING FACTORY WSM & PARTS
AJS 1945-1960 SINGLES MODELS 16 & 18 350cc & 500cc (BOOK OF)
AJS 1948-1956 TWINS MODELS 20 & 30 FACTORY WSM & PARTS
AJS 1955-1965 SINGLES MODELS 16 & 18 350cc & 500cc (BOOK OF)
AJS 1957-1966 SINGLES & TWINS (ALL) FACTORY WSM
AJS 1959-1969 G80CS G85CS & P11 OFF ROAD FACTORY WSM
AJS 1968-1974 STORMER FACTORY WSM & PARTS LIST
ARIEL UP TO 1932 (BOOK OF)
ARIEL 1932-1939 PREWAR MODELS (BOOK OF)
ARIEL 1933-1951 (WORKSHOP MANUAL)
ARIEL 1939-1960 4 STROKE SINGLES (BOOK OF)
ARIEL 1958-1964 LEADER & ARROW FACTORY WSM & PARTS LIST
ARIEL 1958-1964 LEADER & ARROW (BOOK OF)
BMW R26 R27 (1956-1967) FACTORY WORKSHOP MANUAL
BMW R50 R50S R60 R69S (1955-1969) FACTORY WORKSHOP MANUAL
BMW R50/5 R60/5 R75/5 (1969-1973) FACTORY WORKSHOP MANUAL
BRIDGESTONE 90 SERIES FACTORY WSM & PARTS CATALOGUE
BRIDGESTONE 175 SERIES FACTORY WSM & PARTS CATALOGUE
BRIDGESTONE 350 SERIES FACTORY WSM & PARTS CATALOGUES
BSA SERVICE SHEETS MASTER CATALOGUE ALL MODELS 1945-1967
BSA BANTAM D1 TO D7 1948-1966 FACTORY SERVICE SHEETS MANUAL
BSA BANTAM ALL MODELS FROM 1948 ONWARDS (BOOK OF)
BSA BANTAM D14 FACTORY SERVICE MANUAL
BSA DANDY FACTORY WORKSHOP MANUAL (COMPILATION)
BSA SINGLES & V-TWINS UP TO 1926 inc. 1927 SUPPLEMENT (BOOK OF)
BSA SINGLES & V-TWINS UP TO 1930 (BOOK OF)
BSA SINGLES & V-TWINS UP TO 1935 (BOOK OF)
BSA SINGLES & V-TWINS 1936-1939 (BOOK OF)
BSA C10, C11 & C12 1945-1958 FACTORY SERVICE SHEETS MANUAL
BSA OHV & SV SINGLES 250-600cc 1945-1959 (BOOK OF)
BSA C15 & B40 1958-1967 FACTORY SERVICE SHEETS MANUAL
BSA OHV & SV SINGLES 250cc (ONLY) 1954-1970 (BOOK OF)
BSA B31, B32, B33 & B34 1945-60 FACTORY SERVICE SHEETS MANUAL
BSA OHV SINGLES 350 & 500cc 1955-1967 (BOOK OF)
BSA M20, M21 & M33 1945-1963 FACTORY SERVICE SHEETS MANUAL
BSA TWINS A7 & A10 1948-1962 FACTORY SERVICE SHEETS MANUAL
BSA TWINS A7 & A10 1946-1962 (BOOK OF)
BSA TWINS A50 & A65 1962-1965 FACTORY WORKSHOP MANUAL
BSA TWINS A50 & A65 1962-1969 (SECOND BOOK OF)
BULTACO 125cc to 37cc SINGLES 1968-1979 WORKSHOP MANUAL
CZ 125cc to 380cc SINGLES 1967-1974 WORKSHOP MANUAL
DOUGLAS 1929-1939 PREWAR ALL MODELS (BOOK OF)
DOUGLAS 1948-1957 POSTWAR ALL MODELS FACTORY SHOP MANUAL
DUCATI 160cc, 250cc & 350cc OHC MODELS FACTORY WORKSHOP MANUAL
HODAKA 90cc,100cc & 125cc SINGLES 1964-1978 WORKSHOP MANUAL
HONDA 50cc ALL MODELS UP TO 1970 INC MONKEY & TRAIL (BOOK OF)
HONDA 90cc ALL MODELS UP TO 1966 (BOOK OF)
HONDA TWINS & SINGLES 50cc THRU 305cc 1960-1966 (BOOK OF)
HONDA TWINS ALL MODELS 125cc THRU 450cc UP TO 1968 (BOOK OF)
HONDA C100 50cc SUPER CUB O.H.C. 1959-1962 FACTORY WSM
HONDA C110 50cc SPORT CUB O.H.C. 1960-1962 FACTORY WSM
HONDA 50-65-70-90cc O.H.C. SINGLES 1959-1983 WSM
HONDA 100-125cc SINGLES CB/CD/CL/SL/TL 1970-1984 FACTORY WSM
HONDA 125-150cc TWINS C/CS/CB/CA 1959-1966 FACTORY WSM
HONDA 125-160-175-200cc TWINS 1965-1978 WORKSHOP MANUAL
HONDA 250-305cc TWINS C/CS/CB 1961-1968 FACTORY WSM
HOHDA 250-350cc TWINS CB/CL/SL 1968-1973 FACTORY WSM
HONDA 250-360cc TWINS CB/CL/CJ 1974-1977 FACTORY WSM
HONDA 350F & 400F 4-CYLINDER 1972-1977 FACTORY WSM
HONDA 450cc TWINS CB/CL 1965-1974 K0 TO K7 WORKSHOP MANUAL
HONDA 500cc & 550cc 4-CYL 1971-1978 FACTORY WORKSHOP MANUAL
HONDA 750cc SHOC 4-CYL 1969-1978 K0~K8 WORKSHOP MANUAL
HUSQVARNA 125cc to 450cc SINGLES 1965-1975 WORKSHOP MANUAL
INDIAN PONYBIKE, BOY RACER & PAPOOSE ILL PARTS LIST & SALES LIT
J.A.P. ENGINES 1927-1952 & MOTORCYCLES 1934-1952 (BOOK OF)
KAWASAKI TRIPLES 1968-1980 ALL MODELS 250cc to 750cc WSM
MAICO 250cc to 501cc 1968-1978 WORKSHOP MANUAL

MATCHLESS 1931-1939 ALL MODELS 250cc THRU 990cc (BOOK OF)
MATCHLESS 1945-1956 RIGID & SPRING FACTORY WSM & PARTS
MATCHLESS 1945-1956 SINGLES G3 & G80 350cc & 500cc (BOOK OF)
MATCHLESS 1948-1956 TWINS G9 & G11 FACTORY WSM & PARTS
MATCHLESS 1955-1966 SINGLES G3 & G80 350cc & 500cc (BOOK OF)
MATCHLESS 1957-1966 SINGLES & TWINS (ALL) FACTORY WSM
MONTESA 1962-1978 125cc to 360cc ALL MODELS WORKSHOP MANUAL
NEW IMPERIAL ALL SV & OHV FROM 1935 ONWARDS (BOOK OF)
NORTON 1932-1939 PREWAR MODELS (BOOK OF)
NORTON 1932-1947 (BOOK OF)
NORTON 1938-1956 (BOOK OF)
NORTON 1945-1963 MODELS 16H, Big4, ES2, 19 & 50 WSM'S & PARTS
NORTON 1955-1963 MODELS 19, 50 & ES2 (BOOK OF)
NORTON 1948-1970 DOMINATOR TWINS FACTORY WSM'S & PARTS
NORTON 1955-1965 DOMINATOR TWINS (BOOK OF)
NORTON 1960-1970 TWIN CYLINDER FACTORY WORKSHOP MANUAL
NORTON 1970-1975 COMMANDO 850 & 750cc FACTORY WSM
NORTON 1975-1978 MK 3 COMMANDO 850 cc FACTORY WSM
OSSA 1971-1978 125cc, 175cc, 250cc, 310cc WSM
PANTHER 1932-1958 LIGHTWEIGHT MODELS 250 & 350cc (BOOK OF)
PANTHER 1938-1966 HEAVYWEIGHT MODELS 600 & 650cc (BOOK OF)
PENTON-KTM-SACHS 1968-1975 100cc & 125cc WORKSHOP MANUAL
PENTON-KTM 1972-1975 175cc, 250cc & 400cc WSM & PARTS MANUALS
PENTON-KTM 1972-1979 125cc to 400cc ENGINE WSM & PARTS MANUAL
RALEIGH MOTORCYCLES 1919-1933 (BOOK OF)
ROYAL ENFIELD 1934-1946 SINGLES & V TWINS (BOOK OF)
ROYAL ENFIELD 1937-1953 SINGLES & V TWINS (BOOK OF)
ROYAL ENFIELD 1946-1962 SINGLES (BOOK OF)
ROYAL ENFIELD 1948-1962 350cc & 500cc PRE-UNIT BULLET WSM
ROYAL ENFIELD 1948-1963 500cc TWINS FACTORY WORKSHOP MANUAL
ROYAL ENFIELD 1952-1963 700cc TWINS FACTORY WORKSHOP MANUAL
ROYAL ENFIELD 1956-1966 250cc CRUSADER & 350cc NEW BULLET WSM
ROYAL ENFIELD 1958-1966 250cc & 350cc SINGLES (SECOND BOOK OF)
ROYAL ENFIELD 1962-1970 INTERCEPTOR WSM'S & PARTS (Compilation)
RUDGE 1933-1939 (BOOK OF)
SACHS 1968-1975 100cc & 125cc ENGINES WSM & M/CYCLE PARTS LIST
SUNBEAM 1928-1939 (BOOK OF)
SUNBEAM 1946-1957 S7 & S8 (BOOK OF)
SUZUKI 50cc & 80cc UP TO 1966 (BOOK OF)
SUZUKI T10 1963-1967 FACTORY WORKSHOP MANUAL
SUZUKI T20 & T200 1965-1969 FACTORY WORKSHOP MANUAL
SUZUKI TWINS 1962 ONWARDS 125-500cc WORKSHOP MANUAL
SUZUKI GT750 1971-1977 A COMPILATION OF 4 FACTORY WSM's
SUZUKI GT550 1972-1977 A COMPILATION OF 3 FACTORY WSM's
SUZUKI GT380 1972-1977 A COMPILATION OF 3 FACTORY WSM's
TRIUMPH 1935-1949 SINGLES & TWINS (BOOK OF)
TRIUMPH 1937-1961 SINGLES SV & OHV 250cc-600cc + TERRIER & CUB
TRIUMPH 1945-1955 PRE-UNIT 350cc, 500cc & 650cc TWINS WSM No.11
TRIUMPH 1945-1959 TWINS (BOOK OF)
TRIUMPH 1956-1969 TWINS (BOOK OF)
TRIUMPH 1956-1962 PRE-UNIT 500cc & 650cc TWINS WSM No.17
TRIUMPH 1957-1961 UNIT CONSTRUCTION 350-500cc WSM No.4
TRIUMPH 1963-1974 UNIT CONSTRUCTION 350-500cc FACTORY WSM
TRIUMPH 1963-1970 UNIT CONSTRUCTION 650cc FACTORY WSM
TRIUMPH 1968-1974 TRIDENT T150 & T150V FACTORY WSM
TRIUMPH 1971-1973 650cc OIL-IN-FRAME FACTORY WSM
TRIUMPH 1973-1978 750cc BONNEVILLE & TIGER FACTORY WSM
TRIUMPH 1979-1983 750cc T140, TR7 & TR65 FACTORY WSM
VELOCETTE 1925-1970 ALL SINGLES & TWINS (BOOK OF)
VELOCETTE 1933-1952 MOV-MAC-MSS RIGID FRAME FACTORY WSM
VELOCETTE 1953-1960 MAC SPRING FRAME WSM & ILL PARTS LIST
VELOCETTE 1954-1971 MSS-VENOM-THRUXTON-VIPER FACTORY WSM
VILLIERS ENGINE UP TO 1959 INC. 3 WHEELERS (BOOK OF)
VILLIERS ENGINE UP TO 1969 (BOOK OF)
VINCENT 1935-1955 (WORKSHOP MANUAL)
YAMAHA 1961-1967 YA5 & YA6 (WORKSHOP MANUAL & ILL PARTS LIST)
YAMAHA 1963-1976 50cc to 100cc ROTARY VALVE SINGLES WSM
YAMAHA 1968-1971 DT1 & MX SERIES Inc. GYT WORKSHOP MANUAL
YAMAHA 1971-1972 JT1& JT2 (WORKSHOP MANUAL & ILL PARTS LIST)

VELOCEPRESS.com – SCOOTER MANUALS

BSA SUNBEAM SCOOTER WORKSHOP MANUAL 1959-1965
BSA SUNBEAM SCOOTER 1959-1965 (BOOK OF)
LAMBRETTA 1947-1957 ALL 125 & 150cc MODELS (BOOK OF)
LAMBRETTA 1957-1970 LI & TV MODELS (SECOND BOOK OF)
NSU PRIMA 1956-1964 ALL MODELS (BOOK OF)
TRIUMPH TIGRESS SCOOTER WORKSHOP MANUAL 1959-1965
TRIUMPH TIGRESS SCOOTER (BOOK OF)
VESPA 1951-1961 (BOOK OF)
VESPA 1955-1963 125 & 150cc & GS MODELS (SECOND BOOK OF)
VESPA 1955-1968 GS & SS (BOOK OF)
VESPA 1963-1972 90, 125 & 150cc (THIRD BOOK OF)

VELOCEPRESS.com - THREE WHEELER MANUALS

BOND MINICAR THREE WHEELER 1948-1967 (BOOK OF)
BMW ISETTA FACTORY WORKSHOP MANUAL
BSA THREE WHEELER (BOOK OF)
RELIANT REGAL THREE WHEELER 1952-1973 (BOOK OF)
VINTAGE MORGAN THREE WHEELER (BOOK OF)

VELOCEPRESS.com – MOTORCYCLE TECHNICAL BOOKS

1930'S BRITISH MOTORCYCLE CARBS & ELEC COMPONENTS (BOOK OF)
1930'S BRITISH MOTORCYCLE ENGINES (OVERHAUL & MAINTENANCE)
1930'S BRITISH MOTORCYCLE GEARBOXES & CLUTCHES (BOOK OF)
CATALOG OF BRITISH MOTORCYCLES (1951 MODELS)
LUCAS ELECTRONICS BRITISH M/CYCLES REPAIR & PARTS (1950-1977)
MOTORCYCLE ENGINEERING (P.E. Irving)
MOTORCYCLE ROAD TESTS 1949-1953 (Motor Cycle Magazine UK)
SPEED AND HOW TO OBTAIN IT (Motor Cycle Magazine UK)
TUNING FOR SPEED (P.E. Irving)
WIPAC (COMBO) MANUAL NUMBER 3 + M/CYCLE & SCOOTER MANUAL

VELOCEPRESS.com - MOPEDS & MOTORIZED BICYCLES MANUALS

CYCLEMOTOR (BOOK OF)
NSU QUICKLY 1953-1963 ALL MODELS (BOOK OF)
PUCH MAXI N & S MAINTENANCE & REPAIR (3 MANUAL COMPILATION)
RALEIGH MOPEDS 1960-1969 (BOOK OF)

VELOCEPRESS.com - AUTOMOBILE MANUALS BY MAKE

ALFA ROMEO GIULIA WORKSHOP MANUAL 1300 TO 2000cc 1962-1975
ALFA ROMEO GIULIA TECH MANUAL CARBURETED CARS FROM 1962
ALFA ROMEO GIULIA TECH MANUAL FUEL INJECTED CARS FROM 1969
ALFA ROMEO GIULIETTA & GIULIA 750 & 101 SERIES 1955-1965 WSM
AUSTIN-HEALEY SPRITE & MG MIDGET WORKSHOP MANUAL 1958 1971
BMW 600 LIMOUSINE FACTORY WORKSHOP MANUAL
BMW 600 LIMOUSINE OWNERS HAND BOOK & SERVICE MANUAL
BMW 2000 & 2002 1966-1976 WORKSHOP MANUAL
BMW 2500, 2800, 3.0 & BARVARIA WORKSHOP MANUAL
CORVAIR 1960-1969 WORKSHOP MANUAL
CORVETTE V8 1955-1962 WORKSHOP MANUAL
FERRARI HANDBOOK ROAD & RACE CARS (SERVICE/SPECS) 1948-1958
FERRARI 250GT SERVICE & MAINTENANCE by JIM RIFF 1956-1965
FERRARI 250GT & 250GTE FACTORY PARTS AND REPAIR MANUALS
FIAT 500 FACTORY WORKSHOP MANUAL 1957-1973
FIAT 600, 600D & MULTIPLA FACTORY WORKSHOP MANUAL 1955-1969
FORD MUSTANG 1965-1973 TRANSMISSION WORKSHOP MANUAL
JAGUAR E-TYPE 3.8 & 4.2 SERIES 1 & 2 WORKSHOP MANUAL
JAGUAR MK 7, 8, 9 & XK120, 140, 150 WORKSHOP MANUAL 1948-1961
MERCEDES-BENZ 230 SERIES 1963-1968
MERCEDES-BENZ 280 SERIES 1968-1972
METROPOLITAN FACTORY WORKSHOP MANUAL
MGA & MGB OWNERS HANDBOOK & WORKSHOP MANUAL
MG MIDGET TC, TD, TF & TF1500 WORKSHOP MANUAL
PORSCHE 356 1948-1965 WORKSHOP MANUAL
PORSCHE 911 2.0, 2.2, 2.4 LITRE 1964-1973 WORKSHOP MANUAL
PORSCHE 911 2.7, 3.0, 3.2 LITRE 1973-1989 WORKSHOP MANUAL
PORSCHE 912 WORKSHOP MANUAL
PORSCHE 914/4 & 914/6 1.7, 1.8, 2.0 LITRE 1970-1976 WSM
TRIUMPH TR2, TR3, TR4 1953-1965 WORKSHOP MANUAL
VOLKSWAGEN TRANSPORTER, TRUCKS & WAGONS 1950-1979 WSM
VOLVO 1944-1968 ALL MODELS WORKSHOP MANUAL

VELOCEPRESS.com - AUTOMOBILE TECHNICAL BOOKS

HOW TO BUILD A FIBERGLASS CAR
HOW TO BUILD A RACING CAR
HOW TO RESTORE THE MODEL 'A' FORD
MASERATI OWNER'S HANDBOOK
PERFORMANCE TUNING THE SUNBEAM TIGER
SOUPING THE VOLKSWAGEN
SOLEX CARBURETORS (EMPHASIS ON UK & EU AUTOMOBILES)
SU CARBURETORS (EMPHASIS ON UK AUTOMOBILES)
WEBER CARBURETORS (EMPHASIS ON ALFA & FIAT)

VELOCEPRESS.com – AUTOMOBILE BOOKS & GUIDES

COMPLETE CATALOG OF JAPANESE MOTOR VEHICLES
FERRARI 308 SERIES BUYER'S AND OWNER'S GUIDE
FERRARI BROCHURES AND SALES LITERATURE 1968-1989
FERRARI SERIAL NUMBERS PART I - ODD NUMBERS TO 21399
FERRARI SERIAL NUMBERS PART II - EVEN NUMBERS TO 1050
HENRY'S FABULOUS MODEL "A" FORD
MASERATI BROCHURES AND SALES LITERATURE

VELOCEPRESS.com - AUTO RACING BOOKS

BOOK OF THE 1950 CARRERA PANAMERICANA - MEXICAN ROAD RACE
DIALED IN - THE JAN OPPERMAN STORY
VEDA ORR'S NEW REVISED HOT ROD PICTORIAL
LIFE OF TED HORN – AMERICAN RACING CHAMPION

www.VelocePress.com

www.ingramcontent.com/pod-product-compliance
Lightning Source LLC
Chambersburg PA
CBHW080747300426
44114CB00019B/2670